# CRIES OF RESTAURANT CLIENT

## A REFLECTION ON CUSTOMER SERVICE

### F.C. PERALTA

to Chris
Mes—ooo, All the Best

# Contents

—Would you like more bread, sir?
—Thank you.
—Is that... a "yes?"
—Oh, no, thanks. I thought "thank you" always meant "no."
—Of course not, —my wife says. —"Thank you" means "yes."
—Doesn't "thank you" just mean "thank you"?—asked the puzzled server, almost rhetorically.

As it turns out, with a little research I found that "thank you" could indeed mean either yes or no, depending on the local culture or the circumstances. Sometimes it depends on a non-verbal complement, like a facial expression or a hand gesture, to confirm the meaning. My wife and I were both wrong: as in many other circumstances, different people express themselves and interpret information differently, and there was no set rule for the meaning of "thanks" when it comes to accepting or declining an offer. Rules, I have come to learn, are dangerous when not given context and flexibility. This is not a book of rules.

If you have this book in your hands, I presume you attribute significant value to customer service and client satisfaction, and for that, I thank you dearly.

I also give many thanks to my wife, my parents, brothers, and friends, for their enormous support. This book is dedicated to all of you.

# Prologue: In Search of the Holy Grail

December 17 was my last day in corporate finance. At the age of thirty-eight, after eighteen years and numerous financial roles in five companies, I decided to end the Corporate America chapter of my professional life. A few months earlier, I'd had a frank conversation with my boss, who I thanked for the job I had been given not very long before, and explained, to his astonishment, that I had decided I would not spend the next twenty-five years of my professional life sitting in front of a computer and attending meetings. Moreover, I would pursue a new career where I could find self-realization and where I could make a difference.

I packed my bags for culinary school, with the plan of eventually venturing into opening my own restaurant. This was the trade of my choice, an old dream, and I would learn it from the inside out. I went on to learn how a professional kitchen operates, work for reputable chefs, and learn from cooks, managers, servers, dishwashers, and hosts.

I spent a good bit of my spare time in the school's library, researching on culinary arts, restaurant management, interior design, plate presentation, table setting, hospitality service, and food marketing. I was looking for the formula for what makes restaurants successful in a business where so many fail. Professor H. G. Parsa of Ohio State University presented a broadly cited study in 2000, concluding that an astonishing rate of 59 percent of restaurants fail within three years. What would explain why very likeable restaurants go under and some with mediocre food prosper? Could the wisdom be scattered through the bookshelves of the library, waiting to be quilted together and turned into an infallible recipe for success? The more I read, the more frustrated I became; I could find no objective guidance for restaurant triumph.

If the books didn't get to the point, it seemed logical that what I actually needed was some real- life advice from people with proven track records. Many had traveled this road before me, so at every opportunity, I asked chefs, cooks, servers, managers, and restaurant owners about the factors of success for their business.

"Location, Fernando," was the most frequent answer. I understand this as choosing a geographical site where your target segment of the public abounds—your food, of course, being suitable to the taste, habits, fashion, and budget of those people, and such location being convenient for your intended customers: easy to spot, access, park near, or walk to; or strategically located by businesses, entertainment, shopping, gyms, or other places of interest to your target clientele. Quite a straightforward concept, that location plays a major role in determining the success of a restaurant. Some locations are more suitable for a sandwich shop, others for a French bistro. Some locations seem to be doomed to bring every entrepreneur to make acquaintance with a bankruptcy attorney.

Finding the perfect location is not as simple as it sounds because locations don't often come as a one-size-fits-all, like the packs of socks that invariably result in being too small for me. There are great locations, in which you can sell just about anything, but unless you are a psychic, a business genius, or plain lucky to see what nobody else could, these locations are universally acknowledged in the local business communities, and if they become available, they will come at premium cost, which may require you to attain a level of sales that your operation cannot support or to compromise on your ideal square footage or staff size. What you must seek is the location that is perfect for your particular concept and fits well with your business plan. You may want to start by defining your client and food, and then search for the matching location.

Just "Offer great food" was another answer I received. Indeed, I have been to restaurants in odd locations, offering uncomfortable facilities and scarce parking, which turned out to be very successful. People may go out of their way and tolerate all kinds of discomfort and inconveniences if they really want your food. There can be a mystical sense of adventure in braving adversities to find the authentic Lithuanian food served in a remote inn atop the Blue Ridge Mountains. A few cheesesteak places in Philadelphia serve as good examples: cars stand by in double lines, long queues form under open skies vulnerable to the forces of nature, limited and awkward seating is offered, and service isn't particularly friendly. Yet those places are very successful, attracting people from great distances, and feature as travel book spots for tourists. So, indeed, I believe it possible that you could build a reputation out of phenomenal food alone and attract a solid clientele despite many other disadvantageous factors. I just find it perilous to count on that as a business strategy; your potential investors may be likewise skeptical.

The answer "You must have a differentiation" sounds logical, yet vague, and possibly more debatable than the food and location factors. Across the nation we see virtually indistinguishable businesses, selling identical menus, resulting in very prosperous Chinese buffets, hamburger chains, pizza shops, Japanese steakhouses, Mexican restaurants, and finger food bars. It is not without reason that the vast majority of savvy restaurant entrepreneurs prefer to avoid dramatic innovations and to stick to the proven formulas of success.

While I agree that differentiation can be important, in some situations, a predictable menu and environment is expected, rather than eccentric choices of foods and décor. Most people aren't extraordinarily adventurous in their habits. I've met folks who went on trips to splendid sceneries in the Caribbean or Polynesia, and never left the compounds of the all-inclusive resorts to peek at the local culture. Our national parks are loaded with wilderness explorers who go camping in their RVs with full kitchens, laundry rooms, and Blu-ray entertainment. One experienced marketing executive, aware of people's need for an ample comfort zone, told me that, as a rule, he advises the level of innovation to be restrained to no more than 30 percent.

The logic behind the limited innovation is that an overly eccentric menu may be effective in raising curiosity, but might not bring you sufficient regular clients if your food doesn't look or taste like something people would eat habitually. You may also face the risk that your utterly unique food concept catches on, but the fad burns out quickly, like the crêpe houses that popped up everywhere in the seventies, then disappeared as quickly as they came.

I believe the former factors—location and food quality—may play important roles in constructing your differentiation. Your menu might be the same, but better executed. Your ambience may be vanilla, but neater, cleaner, or just closer to public parking. Greater differentiation, when it comes to menu items and ambience, could become more critical if you face such fierce competition that you absolutely must stand out, or if you cater to the affluent and extravagant, who constantly seek new exotic and exquisite dining experiences. In such cases, your uniqueness can trigger word of mouth and stimulate interest. But I believe the same word of mouth could occur if your pizza shop were a touch more comfortable than the one two-hundred feet down the road.

The last piece of feedback came from a chef for whom I have a lot of respect. He told me boldly, "Well, Fernando, you're an educated guy, with your MBA and shit. I'm sure you've heard that service is important, but it is more than that. Trust me, for I've seen a lot in this trade. Bad service will literally destroy your business, no matter how good your food may be." To my surprise, a seasoned chef chose to rank service above all other criteria: location, food, and differentiation.

I took his advice seriously and began my quest to understand the factors that affect the perception of good customer service. I read a few of the many books available on the topic, but quickly realized I wasn't finding the essence I sought or even an effective definition of good customer service. Instead, those books offered knowledge on how to set up a table, assign service zones to servers, schedule reservations, distribute workload, write orders, pair and serve wine, and so on. I found one book with ultimate techniques in upselling and suggestive selling to raise the average check, but not one on actually improving customer satisfaction.

In my reading, I learned that a server must choose a focal point, based on the logical path of approaching a table, and assign each client a clockwise position from that point, so she will remember to whom each order belongs. I also learned that the server should serve a plate from the left, with the left hand, and collect from the right, with the right hand. This allows her to be as unobtrusive as possible and will reduce the risk that a harsh and clumsy elbow move would result in a client with a broken nose, which generally doesn't help much with the tips.

I understood that it makes no sense for servers to bring the wine list before the menu. The client is supposed to make smart choices in pairing wine with food, so he can't logically select the wine before choosing his course. I found out about the trick of leaving the check folder upside down so you'll know the client has looked at it and probably inserted a credit card, once the client follows the natural instinct of laying it back on the table right side up. I discovered that if you add one or two absurdly expensive items for every section of the menu, not expecting, of course, that anyone will order them, you will make all other plates, by means of relative comparison, appear reasonably priced, and clients will be more comfortable with ordering them.

I was not convinced, however, that these practices and techniques were the factors that truly make clients enjoy an exceptional dining experience. While by-the-book service proficiency might impress the critics from Zagat, I don't believe the average client really cares about your wine-serving technique.

Frankly, much of the literature I found about restaurant service focused on operational guidelines rather than client satisfaction. Disappointed, I decided to pursue my own quest to understand customer service. If service is the key to success, I most certainly wanted to have it. I continued to interview people from all walks of life as to what they find pleasurable and bothersome in restaurant service. I found that different flaws displease different people, to widely different degrees. Some people get outraged that the coffee is lukewarm, while other folks barely notice it. The things that delight us, on the other hand, are universal: feeling welcomed, respected, and well-attended.

My research and reflections about service and customer perception evolved into this book. All experiences are real. I was tempted to exaggerate and dramatize for narrative purposes, but I dismissed the idea in order to keep things genuine. I've changed names to protect my friends' privacy.

This book is not meant to unveil guild secrets or portray bombastic scandals. Nor is it a guide to expertise in classical French tableside service. I didn't intend to show the "Wow!" of shocked surprise, but the "Hmm" of common sense. It represents familiar experiences of our daily lives, an occasion to think about how we, as clients, perceive and react to service, and provides an opportunity for businesses to consider a few small adjustments to processes and behaviors that may make a world of difference in attaining better client satisfaction.

# PART 1: THE CLIENT'S VANTAGE POINT

## The Journey, Not the Destination

An intense schedule of business travel, over several years, gave me the opportunity to learn about diverse local cultures and tour some spectacular sites in my sporadic leisure time. As another perk of business travel, all my expenses within the modest budget were reimbursed, allowing me to enlarge my waistline, exploring the pleasures of eating out for every meal. I also experienced the daily life in hotels, which would fulfill my mom's fantasy of never again having to clean the house or repair things.

Frankly, the glamour of saying "I'll be in Paris tomorrow" burns away very quickly. The crude reality includes interminable airport lines, TSA agents patting you down, airplanes clearly not designed for someone who is six foot three, dishonest taxi drivers, overpriced and mildewed hotel facilities, thieves specializing in foreigners, and restaurant menus in Turkish, making a surprise of every meal. Of course, the routine of business trips also includes twelve daily hours in an unfamiliar office, and the deprivation of home comforts, access to personal hobbies, and the company of my friends and family.

Before getting into the specific issues of restaurant service, it is pertinent to address hospitality from the broader perspective of the industry, taking a look at airlines and hotels. I have three reasons for doing this. First, the product being sold in these segments is the service itself, which makes service quality issues more painfully noticeable for clients than the flaws in restaurants. Second, airlines and hotels once held the benchmark that every service business looked up to. Third, hotels and air travel are the first things that come to mind when I hear the word *hospitality*.

Over the years, I've seen fire and rain in these two segments of hospitality. Sadly, bad experiences have been more recurring than good, so let us begin from the ugly side.

If you are a miserable person, chewed up and spit out by the toughness of life, hopelessly depressed, irritable, defensively arrogant, and incapable of the simplest gesture of courtesy, you belong in a major airline. You'll find a support group of infelicity in your peers.

As I make this major generalization, I don't mean to overlook the good and kind people working for airlines, and I apologize for offending your aunt who is a darned good flight attendant. I do remember receiving smiles at the check-in desk, and I've experienced a flight attendant who took the initiative of offering me free extra booze when she noticed that 137 teenagers bound to Disney World wouldn't let me sleep on the overnight flight. But that good care has been the exception, not the typical experience. My point here is to seek the causes behind why so many airline passengers feel like cattle entering a slaughterhouse every time they arrive at the airport, and to consider if any of these impressions may relate to your clients' perception of your restaurant's service.

Airlines employees are infected with a chronic burnout, and the major symptom of this disease is a permanent state of "couldn'tcarelessness" (there's a word for you, Dr. Sir Stephen Colbert). This condition seems to be caused by constant exposure to rude travelers requesting special arrangements, verbally abusing attendants and proclaiming their self-importance, by the lack of employee authority to make decisions and quickly solve the most frequent problems, and by computer systems decades outdated, which are incredibly complicated and invariably result in locked screens.

On the other side of this issue lies the fact that many workers in the airlines, like many servers and cooks, took their jobs as temporary gigs, until they could find something better. Being a flight attendant requires considerable people skills, and some people simply can't keep it up for long. Restaurants will quickly chip and grind the deadwood, while in airlines, tenure and unions protect the inept, who contaminate the whole box of apples by offering inappropriate examples and standards to the novices.

The combination of oblivious employees with corporate bureaucracy results in all major airlines in America being equally difficult to deal with. I've gone through them all, and the average experience is overwhelmingly disappointing. The entire system is messed up, from reservations to handling your bags.

I don't feel outraged only by the frequent delays; what makes me anxious is the lack of information. It would give me greater ease if I knew why the flight was late and if I were given a realistic estimate for departure, rather than see the airport monitor update the departure time in consecutive fifteen-minute increments.

On one flight, I witnessed the drama of a woman assigned to a seat five rows away from her three-year-old son. She asked for help at the check-in desk, the boarding desk, and the flight attendants, but without avail. In a glimpse of common sense I'm ashamed I didn't have, the woman beside me suggested that we both trade our seats so that mother and son could be reunited. I lost my aisle seat, but for a good cause. On an eight-hour flight, it was completely absurd to let the child sit by himself, and none of us in the plane would have been able to sleep.

At another occasion, in Spain, my reservation simply disappeared, in some miscommunication between the two airlines that operated the different legs of our trip back home. The local check-in attendant told me that, regardless of what my printed reservation schedule showed, she couldn't do anything for me because their system didn't show any reservations. On the phone with the Spanish office of the all-American airline, the attendant suggested I had a better chance if I called the airline's office in America, resulting in one hour of international calls to the United States to fix the misunderstanding.

During the most common of issues, when the airline loses your bag—and the opportunities for such are many—the airline doesn't ever seem to know if the luggage actually boarded your flight, was sent on another plane to the same destination, or was simply misplaced randomly on a flight to Akron, OH. If your flight is full, there's a good possibility that someone will have the bags sent on a following flight, due to weight restrictions on the aircraft, but no one is capable of telling you that this will happen or has happened. How can the service desk at the baggage claim area possibly not know which flight the bag was checked into? Don't they scan the tags? Wouldn't loose controls over what bag travels on which flight be a much greater security risk than a tube of Sensodyne in my carry-on luggage? What is this, a bus station in Somalia? I suspect that they do know, but don't share the information with you, because they don't care about you.

Shit happens, of course, but behind every experience of lost luggage and overbooked flights, I met at least one person from the airline who simply didn't give a damn. My despair doesn't come from the fortuities, but from the unbelievable amount of persistence it takes to eventually find an enthusiastic trainee or a competent experienced employee who is willing to try to help.

Now, what better defines the hospitality industry than hotels? Yes, I would like to be welcomed there as I am at my parents' house, but, realistically, I would settle for a place that I can quickly become familiar with and temporarily call home. I'm looking for comfort, privacy, and friendliness, probably in that very order. *Comfort* means clean facilities, reliable hot water, controlled noise and brightness, cable TV, Internet, and a bed somewhere in-between as soft as quicksand and as stiff as a block of concrete. I'm personally obsessed with *privacy*, for I'm protective of my private space to the point of mental disorder. By *friendliness*, I mean I expect to find people at the reception desk who will understand my needs and resolve any issues without giving me a grumpy face or elevating my heart rate.

Unfortunately, hotel service has deteriorated, similarly to what has happened in airlines. Under-qualified and overburdened hotel employees face a tough client crowd, and employees are burning out. Because of the high employee turnover, I often notice the enthusiasm of fresh employees at the counters, many of them working in hospitality for the first time, and wonder how long it will take for the attentive clerk to lose the initiative to place me in a room which is a few more doors away from the family with six children.

I hope you are not thinking, at this point, that my purpose with this book is to rant about things that a regular hospitality employee can't do anything about. On the contrary, my intention is to show that any employee can truly make a difference. With the right spirit, you can do much to make a client happier. On the good side of hospitality, I hold a few simple moments dear in my memory.

One Sunday in Bogotá, Colombia, the hotel receptionist at the Pavilion Suites, a comfortable yet unpretentious four-star hotel, greeted me as I was leaving for a leisurely walk and asked: "Sir, you are leaving without breakfast this morning?"

"Yes, I'm afraid I overslept, and it's now 11:15. I realize it's too late for my eggs Benedict." (I particularly liked their eggs Benedict, well-poached, excellent creamy Hollandaise, crispy potatoes, and a basket of various fresh-baked breads to dip in the abundant sauce.)

"Oh no, sir. Please, by all means, we will be happy to serve you your eggs Benedict. Please come with me."

So I did. Breakfast was to be served until 10:30, and the room rate already included it, so there was no incentive for the hotel to offer this special concession, other than pure zeal for good hospitality and client satisfaction. The gesture pleasantly surprised me, and the eggs came out perfect, as always.

During a different stay at the same hotel, I told another attendant that I would be going away for an extended holiday weekend, so I would be checking out on Friday to be back the following Wednesday. I asked if it would be possible for them to hold most of my luggage in their storage room until I returned, because I didn't need all my stuff with me for the holiday.

"Sir, the hotel will not be fully booked during the period, so there is no need for you to pack your bags. You can leave your belongings right where they are, in your room, until Wednesday, and we will not charge you for the room."

Packing and unpacking every few weeks was a major annoyance of that traveling lifestyle, and being spared that task was priceless. Hotels in Manhattan, for example, actually charge you for holding your luggage in their storage for a few hours, which made me appreciate this hotel's service even more.

At the three-star Blue Tree hotel I often used in São Paulo, Brazil, the staff accommodated my ever-changing reservation arrangements with particular agility and flexibility, keeping me free of worry that I would have to sleep in a cardboard refrigerator box under a bridge or spend hundreds of dollars in reservation change fees, which were hard to justify on my expenses report. One of many times I showed up without reservations, the hotel was full, but they sent me to a competing, fancier hotel down the block and convinced that hotel to charge me the same rate that I would have been charged at my usual hotel. I once wrote a suggestion for Blue Tree to not add bacon or ham to the scrambled eggs, explaining that there were already ham and bacon available on the breakfast buffet, and I never again saw any meat within the eggs. They wrote me a note thanking me for the suggestion, commenting that other vegetarians would probably be pleased too. They were willing to listen and make decisions, especially when it was as simple as making a concession to a vegetarian or keeping the swimming pool open a little later at night, for those of us who stay late at the office. Recently, I asked the Blue Tree for my visit records over the past five years, to complete a puzzle required by the U.S. Immigration Services, informing them of the dates and destinations of all my international travel for the five years preceding my application for citizenship. The hotel e-mailed my records the next morning, apologizing for how long it took.

These small gestures had enormous impact on my satisfaction. They gave me what I needed, sometimes without me even asking for it, and the employees were empowered to make such decisions. Better yet, it didn't cost them anything to keep my stuff in the room, nor were the couple of poached eggs a significant cost for winning my eternal appreciation for their hotel.

This is the spirit of hospitality service that seems to be so frequently overlooked: the attention that makes us feel warmly regarded. This book captures many *do*s and *don't*s of customer service in restaurants, but no other personal experience better illustrates the soul of good service as the good-hearted initiatives at the Pavilion Suites and the Blue Tree. In the restaurant business, servers train in folding napkins and filling water glasses. Such tasks are important, but not the essence of what will make clients feel good. Good hospitality is not a destination; it's the journey of honestly, sincerely, and truly caring about clients' pleasure. That can't be accomplished by following a set of procedures; it comes from a state of mind, a creed that the customer's happiness matters.

# Successful People

As I look into the biographies of famous successful people, and even of inconspicuous business rising stars that I've encountered through my career, I rarely find that they obsessed over making money. Renowned chefs like Thomas Keller, who started in his profession as a dishwasher and rose to be nominated the best chef in America in 1997, or his former pupil, Grant Achatz, who made a courageous move to go on his own at the early age of thirty-one and opened a very successful restaurant (Alinea was named the best restaurant in America by *Gourmet* magazine in 2006, one year after opening), display an urge for uniqueness and excellence. Exceptional professional athletes, like Tiger Woods and Rafael Nadal, seek technical perfection. Scientists seek a breakthrough, like Einstein, who had multiple job applications for high school teaching denied and persevered until his general theory of relativity was acknowledged, or Isaac Newton, born to a family of farmers and considered a below-average student for most of his childhood, to later publish the general principles of gravitation and mechanics that are still mostly current. True statesmen like Churchill and Gandhi stand for a cause and artists of the caliber of the violinist Joshua Bell and the cellist Yo-Yo Ma pursue virtuosity. Extraordinary people are motivated by an urge to make a difference, winning, perfecting, standing out, or pushing their limits of physical strength, skills, and creativity. Money often serves as a secondary incentive.

I'm not stating that all successful people display extraordinary traits of character. In fact, while some are altruistic, others would step on their mothers' throats to climb a step. But wealth alone is frequently not the incentive for their successes. Compulsive obsession, the willingness to leave an impression, or simply plain vanity often precedes money in what they value.

I've also found that, more often than not, fortune sooner or later rewards the combination of talent and determination, but not so much when money is the major motivation. Looking back, I now realize that my career evolved more successfully when I focused on my work rather than when I was focused on my career. I had become too concerned with my promotions and paycheck, which was a good sign that my profession didn't excite me anymore, accelerating my urge to switch careers to something where passion would again motivate me.

When you focus too much on money, you may overlook many other important factors, and you may be susceptible to making bad decisions based on short-term gains. For example, if you manage a restaurant from a short-term gross profit perspective alone, you may be tempted to save on the quality of ingredients or service staff, to underpay employees, to choose below-average purveyors, to use inappropriate construction materials, or to price yourself out of the market. Whereas if you focus on quality, employee satisfaction, and good service, you may have a better chance of finding a long-term loyal clientele that will appreciate your efforts.

I once worked for a company that was a leader in electronic controls. We often cost twice as much as the competition, and yet clients continued to choose us, because we had an unmatched reputation for excellence in engineering and relentless customer service. We would often step in and take care of problems that we clearly didn't cause, resulting from mistakes of various other parties involved in the project. When someone else messed up, we would ship a team of our own engineers to solve whichever issue might have arisen, at our own expense. This drove me nuts as a finance person. I had numerous arguments with engineers, salespeople, and the field services department, convinced that the practice was inefficient and abused by our business partners, forcing us to inflate our product prices. In reality, our clients willingly paid the premium for peace of mind, knowing that our product was more reliable and that we'd stand by our clients without reservations. Our good faith was constantly abused, but overall, and regardless of my belief that we could have managed things differently, the company was very successful and held solid profits.

I address the money factor early in this book because I don't want it to be a taboo or an obstacle between you, the business, and me, the client. I'm not naïve. I understand the importance of cash flow, the need to pay your purveyors and staff and still make a profit, to keep the business going. As a business, you must track the seat occupancy, schedule the appropriate number of servers and cooks per shift, well-manage your inventory, and price your food intelligently. I simply suggest you keep money in its due place in your scale of values and priorities: as the result of your actions, not the main motivation.

One classical example distortion of the approach to money is found in pricing. Many restaurants use the formula of multiplying their food costs by a factor, often between three and four, to determine their food price. In this methodology, an item that costs $2 in ingredients would be priced at $8. The problem with that practice is that it is entirely focused on you, the restaurant, not me, the customer. More relevant than the price markup factor is that you study your clientele, current or potential, and your competition, and price your food from those two factors. The knowledge of your clients' price point will determine the menu you can afford to serve. You can use the cost multiplier to verify your profitability, but looking only at this multiplier could lead you to price food at a level that is too expensive for your clients or, and I hate to say this, to leave money on the table, for your clients might be willing to pay more.

Another reason I disagree with the practice of marking up your costs is I shouldn't pay for your inefficiency. If you have too much inventory waste and spoilage, if you hired too many people or are paying too much in interest for your debt because you used your credit cards instead of an SBA loan to finance your business, I don't want to be the one to dig you out of your troubles through overpriced food, especially if your competition is lean and mean. Nobody has ever said that this is an easy business to be in.

Money is not your business; it's the result of your business. It serves also as a tool for tuning your operations to be at the quality your clients want and at the cost you can afford. Monitor the numbers of your restaurant, like a pilot who checks the many gauges in the cockpit, but remember that the main goal is not to save fuel, but to sell seats, fly the plane safely, and arrive on time. If you do not focus most of your attention on your customer service, menu, and food quality, a red light should come on in the cockpit.

Quality-conscious restaurants aren't only found in the high end of fine dining; some very successful businesses cater to those of us who are more watchful of our spending. Many sandwich shops, buffets, and simpler establishments serve honest food for palatable prices, while taking that extra step with customer service. Even restaurants that succeed in highly price-sensitive markets don't necessarily build their reputations on the low price, but on their quality. I don't usually hear people saying, "Hey, man, I found this really cheap Chinese buffet." Instead, I hear, "Hey, I found this excellent buffet, which is also very reasonably priced at lunch time." Restaurants that focus too much of their marketing efforts in divulging their promotional prices make me suspicious. Do they have nothing to say about their food? Even though I like to pay less whenever possible, I don't like to think of my stomach as a fuel tank waiting to be filled with the cheapest gasoline available.

See, I'm not suggesting that higher quality means buying black truffles from France or the purest saffron from Kashmir. If all you serve is spaghetti *aglio e olio*, it costs you less than $1.00 in ingredients to serve a $7.00 plate, so the least you can do is use better quality pasta from premium durum, genuine extra virgin olive oil, and fresh garlic. Have some decent Parmesan or Pecorino to offer, and you are good to go. When you cook with respect and choose ingredients carefully, the difference is noticeable, and you can still be making over 80 percent gross margin using good stuff. But too many restaurants unfortunately choose blended oil, the cheapest pasta available, and the nasty garlic that comes in oiled jars. You may still have a market, but there won't be a queue outside your door. Everything is relative, as Einstein once said. If your clientele is willing to pay no more than $10 per plate, you can't serve a risotto of exotic mushrooms that cost $15 per pound, for you would have to serve an insipid risotto or lose money. You could, however, serve a decent spring vegetables risotto, blending vegetables of different costs. Plan your menu to serve the best food possible within your clients' budgets.

There might be times when things get tough, and you will need to further trim your costs. We customers understand, but we have expectations somewhat proportional to what you charge, meaning that if you charge a premium price, your food should also be top quality. Clients will comprehend that in days of economic hardship, you may trim your menu or reduce staff. At some point, however, your savings initiatives will significantly damage your service and food. If your cuts cost you clients, no savings will be enough. Take a hard look at your business model and figure out if you can make money at all and how much would be a realistic expectation. You may realize that your model doesn't work and, instead of losing your identity, you may want to re-launch your business, maybe as a significantly different one.

If you are a server, you certainly know the range of money you can make on a given night. In fact, many servers will call in before their shifts and get a feel for how many reservations there are, to decide whether they will be sick that evening. Some may focus too much of their attention on the probable high tippers or somehow convince the hostess to sit the right profile of people at their tables. Most waiters believe that middle-aged men, accompanied by women other than their wives, leave the best tips. They also expect richer elderly to tip well, but seniors who rely on Social Security and younger folks are expected to be more conscious of their spending. In the long run, the practice of hand-picking your clients will turn against you. Neglected clients might tip even less than expected, or worse, not return, causing the restaurant to turn fewer tables, which is bad for everyone. Your peers will quickly figure out your game, and they will sabotage you. They'll misplace your stuff or take one of your dishes from an eight top and give it to another table, making the rest of the order get cold or dry. They won't cover for your sickness and emergencies, will not help with your tables when you're in the weeds, and will trash-talk you to the owner and manager. For you, too, I advise against greed; do the best you can within the conditions, and be consistent. Your average income will be more reliable, and your job will continue to be yours.

# Bureaucrats

A large group of friends and I once stayed at a bed and breakfast that had rules. Fritz, the owner, was a descendant of Swiss immigrants from the German side of Switzerland, where every rule is praised as if Moses brought it down from Mount Sinai.

In addition to the expected rules for check-in, check-out, and breakfast schedule, we found many peculiar guidelines for our stay, such as a code of conduct for the use of the bathroom: We would be provided one soap and one roll of toilet paper per stay, hot showers were not to last longer than 10 minutes, and male guests were to urinate in a seated position after 9:00 p.m., after which time flushing was also disallowed. Towels, not bed linen, would be changed every two days, when the housekeeper would perform limited room service duties. In our chalet's kitchen, we found a sign stating that under no circumstances could the housekeeper be requested, persuaded, or bribed to wash dishes and cookware. OK, maybe the sign didn't use the word *bribed*. Bills were to be settled in cash, and change greater than twenty dollars could not be guaranteed.

Fritz was an odd-looking fellow, the kind of person who stares silently for long periods of time, either being lost in thoughts or searching for a lost thought. His face displayed the kind of expression you often see on the television, in the photo of a suspect of a university shooting. He roamed the premises in the company of a German shepherd, the dog being significantly more affable than the owner. Fritz didn't smile or entertain much, but he was kind enough to switch on the sauna for us at a time of the day he found to be oddly untimely. Then, not one to let energy go to waste, he decided to join us, unveiling more of his Swiss secrets than we wished to see. On a wall, outside the sauna, he kept handmade charts of the precipitation in the region for the previous 20 years, a sight that discouraged us from ever making any small talk to him about the weather.

In the morning, he knocked persistently on guests' doors at 8:00 a.m. to remind us of breakfast, which effectively gets your heart rate pumped up to start the day. My girlfriend woke up distressed and disoriented, but she promptly decided that breakfast wasn't such a bad idea, after all. I mumbled profanities, indicating that I'd like to sleep a bit longer. A few moments later, my companion returned in complete frustration and recited back my unprintable words. The breakfast for two, which was included in the room rate, was to be served to the duo in a single seating, and not in two separate instances.

To our good fortune, we didn't face any situation during that trip that demanded special arrangements for Fritz to accommodate within his rules, so that, other than for the frustrated attempt for an individualized breakfast, we weren't much annoyed, but rather found Fritz's obsessions anecdotally entertaining, in a perverted kind of way.

But who among us can't relate to an experience where the rules prevented your perfectly reasonable request from being met? "Sorry, we do not allow any substitutions to the menu," or, "We can't seat a deuce at that larger table by the window even on an empty Tuesday lunch."

Sometimes the Service Representative will even tell me that she would gladly help me if she could, but I turned out to be a victim of the system. The computer system:

—Sir, you cannot use your voucher for this trip because you have already used it.

—Ma'am, this is a voucher I received for volunteering out of an overbooked flight on Christmas Eve. I used it last week to book a flight three weeks from today, which I now realize I will not be able to board. Due to work-related issues, I cannot travel that date, so I need to change the date of my flight, keeping the itinerary the same.

—I can give you a new reservation, but you cannot use this voucher toward it.

—Why?

—Because you already used it.

—But I haven't flown… The scheduled flight is on a future date. I just need to change that date, keeping all else equal, including the usage of the voucher.

—We can't do that. The computer shows that you already used the voucher.

—When?

—It was used toward your current reservation.

—The one I want to change?

—Correct.

—But I won't fly that date, hence the service won't be rendered, and the voucher won't be used. I want to change the reservation, pay the changing fee and the difference in fare, and use the voucher in this changed reservation.

—We can't do that because the voucher has already been used.

—Ma'am, does this make any sense to you?

—That's what the computer shows.

—Is there anyone else I can discuss this case with?

This agonizing phone conversation lasted just short of two hours, with two attendants and two supervisors, followed by a letter to customer service, where they finally made a resolution for a one-time exception, never to be conceded again, allowing me to use the voucher for a "second time." This was the last time I'd ever volunteer out of an overbooked flight, I then promised my patient wife.

It used to be that "The rules are the rules." Now it's that "The system won't allow me to process your request." Either way, we clients are victims of processes overpowering common sense. The fact that something displays on your screen doesn't necessarily make it right. I want you to have the empowerment and sagacity to apply logic and your best judgment to find a way to solve my problem.

So I can't remember my PIN, and my pet's name, which answers the secret question, might be in upper case or misspelled in the system. I just want to pay my bill, which is due today. If I pay it online, it will only be credited the next day, and I'll be charged a late fee. In fact, I hereby authorize you to receive payment from anyone who is determined to pay my bill. If anyone calls who knows my account number, my Social Security number, and the spelling of my name, and insists on paying my bill, please take the money and thank him on my behalf.

Policies can be the archenemy of customer service. Policies and rules are generally designed to address the business' operation, not my satisfaction as a client. I can appreciate that you can't operate in an anarchical environment, but try to keep my comfort and needs in mind and overrule the policies if need be.

As an owner or manager, please make sure to design your processes to leave room for common sense. I want you and your employees to do what is right, logical, and reasonable. Use your power and make "common sense" the new rule.

If, like Fritz, you use too many bizarre policies, rules and restrictions, I'll probably look to go eat somewhere else, where I can be more at ease.

# Organs

Human bodies have twenty-three organs. The name comes from the Latin *organum*, meaning "instrument." Most work in conjunction with other organs, forming systems: respiratory, cardiovascular, digestive, neurological, reproductive. Everyone has specific duties, which, when in good health, will be diligently accomplished. Our lungs, for example, work as part of the respiratory system and in conjunction with the cardiovascular system in the incredibly complex process of oxygenating our cells. The air goes through the nose or mouth, then the glottis and trachea, to arrive in the lungs, where the bronchi filter the air and break it down into small molecules of gases, which the alveoli disperse into the bloodstream. Once in the blood, which the heart pumps through the astounding distance of 60,000 miles of vessels, oxygen will hitchhike with a protein called hemoglobin, which manages the cellular exchange of molecules of oxygen for molecules of carbon dioxide. Cells depend on the delivery of oxygen for a chemical reaction that produces energy for all of our bodily functions. On the way back, the hemoglobin brings carbon dioxide to the lungs, to be discarded in a subsequent exhalation.

Another complex process takes place in the digestive system, where our mouths start the process by chewing foods into smaller pieces, adding moisture and enzymes that start breaking down carbohydrates. Once pushed down the esophagus, food reaches the stomach, where hydrochloric acid and enzymes begin to digest protein. The result is then pushed into the small intestine, where most of the digestion is completed and many nutrients are absorbed. At this point, digestion wouldn't be possible without the enzymes produced in the pancreas and the liver. The liver, much like an overworked, underpaid, and underappreciated Peruvian dishwasher, performs numerous functions critical for our normal operation, as long as it's not intoxicated with excessive tequila or Pisco, in which case it will take a day off and really screw our bodily functions. About eight hours later, waste is transported to the large intestine, which is chubbier, but four times shorter than the small intestine, where it will rest for up to eighteen hours until it knocks on the rectum's door, sometimes quite loudly and possibly at an inappropriate moment, announcing that it's ready to leave the hospitality of your body and rejoin nature. Wasteful liquids are filtered into the bladder, where they're held, in my case not for very long, until the opportunity to disperse it.

As you can see, a lot is happening in the body at all times, though you don't really give it much thought or appreciation. A restaurant, too, to function as a healthy organism, depends on the good operation and synchronicity of many components. Until I became a cook, I wasn't aware of the entire chain of events that occur for a plate of food to reach my table. I was oblivious to the work done by the chef, prep cooks, grill cooks, busboys, and the servers—not to mention those who produced, packaged, and delivered the ingredients. Even as cooks, we still take our comrades' work for granted. We, however, certainly notice each other when someone screws up and now three plates are drying under the heat lamps while someone is re-plating position two, who had requested sauce on the side.

Only when the liver calls in sick, or gets deported to Peru, do we appreciate all its hard work: synthesizing amino acids from digested proteins, transforming carbohydrates into glucose, metabolizing triglycerides and cholesterol, producing hormone IGF-1, bile, and plasmin, an essential coagulation factor; detoxifying the digestive system, regulating the levels of insulin in the blood, and storing glucose, vitamins A, D, and B12, and the minerals iron and copper. The liver is critical, just like the dishwasher in a restaurant. A busy restaurant cannot operate healthily without an efficient person at the dishwasher station; it's a nightmare.

Clients, too, take customer service all for granted, just like we don't pay attention to whether our hearts are pumping. The sad but unequivocal truth for people in this business is that good service will be unnoticed, most of the time, but clients will undoubtedly detect your errors. If the server took the order correctly and brought it promptly, at the right temperature, and without spilling half of the sauce on the table, the client didn't notice anything out of the ordinary. If you exchanged a plate with table seventeen or forgot to bring the appetizers before the entrée, clients become aware of service issues. Bad service may cause you to lose a client, while good attention may not earn you many compliments or a 30% tip. Nevertheless, your goal should be to ensure that everything runs seamlessly, smoothly, and to aspire to noticeable excellence.

Good customer service must be built on the foundation of a healthy and functional organism, which you ought to cultivate well to demand exceptional performance. Every employee is important, should be well cared for, and must learn to work as a team, so that everyone can perform at their best and with good synergy.

# Be My Guest

In this book, I preferred the use of the word *client* instead of *customer*. *Customer* indicates a transaction, while *client* implies a relationship. In the companies I worked for, we chose to refer to our customers as *clients* as a way of reminding salespeople, operational staff, and administrative staff that we expected to be doing business with these companies for the long run, so ethical and attentive services and support were in order.

Because restaurants are classified in the hospitality industry, some people like to call their clients "guests." As a client, I don't like the way that sounds, for it seems like patronizing marketing silliness.

I'm friends with a lovely couple fortunate enough to live in Paris. Even though they know well enough the annoying pain-in-the-ass kind of person I am, they would happily receive me in their nice apartment, offer me a bedroom, leave me brewed coffee in the morning when they leave for work and I'm still sleeping, and allow me to mess up their bathroom without expecting any rewards. To me, that's what the guest relationship is.

Of course you want your clients to receive the same warm and welcoming feel you give to the guests that come to your home, but the relationship has a fundamental difference: a restaurant is mercantile. Calling clients "guests" sounds as cynical as the New York City museums that don't charge admission, but instead solicit a suggested admission donation in the amount of $20.

Unless you operate a hotel or bed and breakfast, where the term "guest" sounds more convincing, I suggest that you avoid this euphemistic terminology. Think of me as a client, and let us develop our relationship on those grounds. It implies a contract, in which you are rendering services and I'm paying for them, and expectations fall on both parts: a certain quality and safety of the food, and a full payment of the check plus taxes and a minimum 15 percent gratuity.

*Client* is a good word; it doesn't diminish your warm and courteous hospitality.

# You Must Wait

On a cold Friday night in February after a rather intense week at work, I had plans for cooking something simple at home: whole wheat fusilli with fresh tomatoes in small dice, onions, garlic, fresh basil, Pecorino Romano, and spinach *chiffonade*. This very flavorful dish is quick and easy to make and quite popular with my friends. The only important rule for this (and most things you cook with onions) is that the onions must be the first thing to hit the oiled pan, and they ought to be lightly browned, to develop flavor. The tomatoes contain a lot of moisture, and after you add them, the onions will not caramelize any longer. Many chefs will choose canned tomatoes, since good ripe tomatoes are hard to find, especially in the middle of the winter. The overpriced ones found at the supermarket were picked while green, endured long travels, and did not develop a full taste, leaving the sauces a bit too acid. I like them fresh, anyway, and if I can't get enough sweetness from cooking the tomatoes a little longer, I can always add a half teaspoon of Agave or a bit of shredded carrots to the sauce. Fusilli's shape is designed for retaining the sauce, and Barilla has accomplished respectable quality on their whole-wheat version. It takes about twenty minutes from startup to cleanup, if you start the sauce as you boil water for the pasta, and I'd soon be in front of the TV, tray on my lap, popping some minimal brain activity thriller into my Blu-ray, perfect for closing a demanding week. My wife will actually pay attention to the plot, so I can count on her to remind me which guy carried a briefcase full of money at the beginning of the movie.

Just as I was working on my *mise en place*, pulling things out of the fridge, a friend called, wanting to go out for dinner. I whined, and he knew it takes effort to get me out of the comfort of my pajama pants. He calls us old and lazy. "It's not even in the city, Fernando," he said, knowing that a long drive in heavy traffic and a $30 parking fee do not make a good start for my vision of a relaxing Friday night. I eventually conceded, and off we went.

The destination was an Italian place, fairly large, resembling casual restaurant chains, although this one was independent. The relatively new place had done a good job reforming and decorating. The building had previously been a bar/restaurant with an unremarkable name and atmosphere. Toward the agonizing end, the previous business tried live music and dancing nights, which only made things worse. Possibly due to the choice of band and music, they attracted older crowds, in their later fifties and sixties. This demographic tends to eventually scare away the younger crowds in their twenties and thirties, and this caused the strategy to be self-destructing. I'm certain that most guys, even in their fifties, don't really like to dance, so they won't do it very often unless it's a barter for the weekend golf outings permit. Most of us guys make use of dance for the very specific objective of picking up girls, and we see no need to continue to go through the trouble of dancing thereafter with our significant others. I only know one couple that goes out to dance regularly, and I have a theory as to why: she talks compulsively and uninterruptedly like no one I ever saw. Like playing the harmonica, she must alternate inhalation and exhalation through the vocal chords, so you never have a chance to interject. Given the option of two hours of uninterrupted listening at a restaurant table, I suppose he, wisely, decided that dancing isn't too bad after all.

So, the older bachelors at the bar wistfully watched the girls in their twenties, the married dancing guys also enjoyed inoffensively checking out the chicks, but when the young girls realized most of the men were much older, they freaked out and vanished, causing all single guys, young and not so much so, to also seek another venue. The remaining dancing couples weren't enough to cover the fixed costs. The place closed, not lasting much longer than the business before them in that building, which had intended to be a knockoff of Red Lobster.

The new owners, if nothing else, gave the Italian place an identity. There's a nice counter bar, two brick pizza ovens, the usual Italian dishes, and a seasonal terrace. The main dining area is decorated as a countryside piazza, and it's fairly pleasant. I'm not so sure about the quality of the food, but I really go there for the beer. It used to be relatively inexpensive. Nowadays, their prices are catching up with some more serious restaurants, and I will have to rethink that venue as a dining choice altogether. At $16 for a plate of vegetarian pasta, I could actually get good pasta at a better restaurant.

It was pretty full that evening, proving that a location that seemed doomed to failure can indeed be salvaged. I parked in a narrow spot, which nobody wanted, given the odds that one or both patrons parked to the right and left, when entering their vehicles and after having a few drinks, would give a nice door bang against whoever chose to park there. I usually practice defensive parking, choosing to be closer to expensive cars, hoping the owner will care for her own door, parking beside handicapped spots, which rarely are occupied, or favoring being closer to passenger doors than to driver doors, betting on the possibility that people will be by themselves. I felt lazy, and the northern wind was whistling.

I heard the words "half-hour wait." *Hmm… Deep breaths.* If I'm told that I have to wait fifteen minutes, it bothers me. If it's thirty minutes, it bothers me quite a lot, and you'd better be the rebirth of Ferran Adrià's elBulli to make me wait forty-five minutes or more. Unless I'm willing to endure climbing the hills of Cataluña on bare feet and get a second mortgage on my house to try the alchemy of molecular gastronomy, when I hear "one-hour wait," I will turn away and look for somewhere else to eat. At that point, my wife's lecture on my impatience is less bothersome than the wait. Half an hour is about the limit of my patience for waiting for a meal of average-quality industrial pasta with canned tomato sauce. We stayed.

We waited standing; no stools were available at the bar, and the waiting area was full. It appears that the bar has the best flat-screen TVs in town for the NHL, and the Flyers were doing alright that season. I gave up on trying to make my way across to get a beer.

I started to entertain myself by looking at people in the waiting area. One gentleman rested on a rather enlarged gluteus, taking a space that would comfortably fit three people. I don't say that to pick on him, for I have found the majority of stouter people to be very pleasant folk. I wished he'd take better care of his health, though. He'd evidently decided to take on Michael Phelps' diet of eight thousand daily calories, without going through the trouble of exercising at the level of an Olympic athlete. I imagined he must've been enjoying life, so I let him be; life is indeed too short. So my attention turned to two women who set their handbags beside them on the bench. I ground my teeth. Where I come from, women have the superstition that handbags should never go on the floor, even if the marble was just polished by a Vatican Swiss guard, then blessed and kissed by the pope himself. A handbag on the floor means bad luck and money loss. Personally, I prefer superstitions that won't make seating unavailable for people who are waiting, standing on their feet.

I was clearly getting impatient. The dial in my watch wasn't spinning fast enough. I fidgeted as I pretended to listen to my friend's detailed comparison between the Toyota minivan and the Volvo XC90 he just test drove, and my eyes started to wander around the restaurant. Suddenly it hits me: *Hey! What's that? Are those tables empty?! I guess they are! Three of them, right there.* See, my stomach was getting ready to auto-digest itself. I had been ready to cook about an hour before and hadn't eaten anything since my lunch salad. Why weren't we being escorted to one of the empty tables? I was pretty sure they don't take reservations there, so it couldn't have been that. Would there be a policy dictating that every client must wait at least thirty minutes to be seated? Does this give the owner the perception of greater importance, that seats in his restaurant were disputed like those four $300 laptops at Best Buy on Black Friday? Did they want to ensure that I'm hungry enough that the mozzarella sticks will taste like beluga caviar fresh from the Caspian Sea?

Word was that they hadn't seated me yet because they weren't ready for me. The house customer service standard is that servers take care of no more than four tables; five if two are deuces. That day, two servers had called in sick. For some servers I know, that would mean they had the party of a lifetime the previous night and were in hypoglycemic comas, too hung over to reach the shower, or too embarrassed to show up for work and face their peers after they sobered up and recalled the events. The two hostesses did show up for work, so I presumed they missed the party, but none of them would help with the tables, possibly because it would damage their recent nail jobs.

Well, folks, I'd had it; it drives me nuts to see empty tables while people are waiting to sit. Even if service would be slow, I'd much rather wait in a seated position. I mentioned leaving, but my wife and friends convinced me that everywhere else would be full and it was too cold outside.

So there is the dilemma: would you rather sit your clients at the table and let them face a longer-than-normal wait for their orders to be taken, or leave them standing? I acknowledge that the human brain has mechanisms to retain good experiences and be condescendingly forgetful of the bad ones, as in waiting ninety minutes at Walt Disney World for an underwear-soaking ride on Splash Mountain and leaving the park with a smile on our faces. Indeed, I barely remember the long lines from the first time I hit the theme parks in Orlando, but I certainly remember the rides. I almost see the point of making people wait so the experience will be the best possible when they are finally served, but I'm not sure I buy this concept. Also, I believe you can handle the wait in different ways or make it less painful:

- Make the waiting area a little more comfortable. The seats don't have to be an award-winning design of cast iron, but inviting seating with a bit of cushioning and back support. Maybe you can also block the freezing air that enters every time someone goes out for a fag or returns in a cloud of smoke. Perhaps add another few seats to the waiting area as your restaurant becomes more popular.

- Bring us some water or soda and something to munch. Some Texas-themed steakhouses do it with shell peanuts, which can also be found at the waiting area of Five Guys. I believe that a handful of reheated tortilla chips and ten fluid ounces of soda are a marginal cost compared to a $35-per-person check, and it will distract me for a while. Maybe one of the hostesses can help with that.

- Take me to the empty table and tell me the *truth*: that you are understaffed because three of your servers flew to Thailand with a Red Cross humanitarian mission to aid the victims of a tsunami, and then apologize for expected delays, but, you know, the entire east coast of the Gulf of Thailand was devastated, and humanity comes first. Then take my drink orders, bring me some bread with the drinks, and off you go to take care of the other tables.

- Don't let me see the empty tables. They've gotta be way in the back, blocked from my sight. Hide them with a barricade of tomato cans or the photo collage of the owner's last trip as a single to New Orleans's Mardi Gras.

- Owner and managers: give the waiters a bonus for picking up the increased work volume and show them appreciation for putting up the effort. Motivate them. I, too, don't like to pick up the work that some lazy slop left behind, and I would certainly like some kind words along with some dough. Sure, the servers will make more in tips, but they also have to be twice as fast, carry twice as many trays, and deal with twice as many tough clients.

We eventually sat, the dining experience was far less memorable than my first ride in the Splash Mountain, and I didn't forget the waiting. On the upside, I found my car undented in the parking lot, and that counts for something.

# Laziness

I'm proudly lazy. Not the irresponsible and inconsequential kind of lazy, but of the type who will pursue the route of lesser effort for equal results. I, for example, can dice vegetables with decent consistency, but the Robot Coupe does it thirty times faster, so what's the point in using my knife? Pride?

As you may have realized by looking at all devices we use in our daily lives, laziness is arguably the major motivator of all big inventions. Otherwise we'd still be traveling great distances barefoot and carrying heavy loads on top of our heads. Or we would still be cultivating land without tractors or hunting beasts with stones and bones for our survival. Since most of us nowadays have atrophied muscles, we now gladly walk very little between the parking lot and our desks and from the couch to the fridge. And back to the couch, and back to the fridge...

The comfort of our days is truly wondrous. Which ancient prophet would have foreseen that we'd be able to attain food without even standing up, just driving through? Too bad we are getting obese, diabetic, and hypertensive, causing life expectancy to potentially drop for the first time, of all the generations for which we have ever measured life expectancy. In this brave new world, it seems that some of the children born at the turn of the century might not be around for too long to enjoy these fabulous times.

So I admit that I, too, enjoy the wonders of comfort and technology, and I like finding ways of greater efficiency and less effort to attain the same objective. Strangely, I'm also obsessive and compulsive, the kind that believes nothing is ever good enough and nothing is ever complete. Here's how this works: when I have something unpleasant to do, I will procrastinate for as long as possible. I'll first do the things that I find more enjoyable, get distracted with unimportant stuff, and when the consequences of further delay seem to be serious enough, I'll eventually get to the boring and laborious tasks, but not without looking for a way in which it can be accomplished more quickly and easily.

For instance, every time I moved, I repainted all the walls in the new house. It's the least expensive and most high-impact reform you can possibly do, where you get a lot of visual bang for your bucks. I always made sure to complete painting before my furniture and the new carpets arrived, so I had a clear deadline to abide by. The daily painting routine would start with me dragging my feet around the house with a cup of coffee in hand, choosing which wall to begin with that day, and how difficult the task would be. How many corners would I need to go through—corners of different colors slow me down, compared to long flat walls—and what color already covered the wall (which would determine how many coats of paint would be necessary). The most tedious task, by far, is masking ceiling junctures, corners, and baseboards. I've been practicing, but I still lack the fine motor skills to cut in freehand with a brush—I'm told that the secret is to use very little paint on the brush. I leave the room in need of the most masking for last, always with the hope that my wife will take care of the masking, as well as the kitchen's dark blue wall that must be painted white. Who the hell paints a kitchen dark blue, for heaven's sake?

Then, a certain transformation takes place in my brain: once the can is open, the roller moist in paint, the music playing on the boom box, and I have enough cold beer to get through the day, I am unstoppable. My wife will get hungry and go out for food in one of her several breaks, but I will be going for twelve, fourteen hours, doing as many coats as necessary to be perfect and working much longer than the contractor I hired to paint the windows' shutters. (Those guys balance on ladders better than I do.)

When it comes to eating at restaurants, my lethargy manifests another way: I'm hesitant to go out for dinner. If I'm convinced I have enough food and drinks at my house to satisfy a fair number of guests, my first reaction is always in favor of entertaining at home. But some friends insist on going out. Given the fact that I love to eat and drink, have solid appreciation for the restaurant business, and have some discretionary money budgeted for leisure, I should feel more excited about going out for dinner, yet I'm reluctant. Why?

For one, I'm tired of bad restaurant food. More specifically, chain restaurants' style of food. I confess that I'm no saint when it comes to choosing and ordering, but I do have a conscience, which usually only comes to action after the fact or via psychic alerts in my mind of what is going to happen, as I listen to the invitation on the phone. As the night unfolds, I will eat three mozzarella sticks with marinara sauce at 130 calories apiece, another 950 calories from the eggplant Parmesan served with pasta, 470 calories from three pints of beer, and 740 calories from half of a brownie with hot fudge and ice cream. I struggle to control my weight, and 2,550 calories in one meal don't go unnoticed. When I get home, I can feel my digestive system struggling, and I have a restless night's sleep. Once I sit at the table, I'm hypnotized by the seduction of junk foods. For that, I can blame the areas of the brain known as pleasure centers, because they process and react to sensations of pleasure. These areas enjoy deep-fried junk in the same manner that they are stimulated by chocolate, cigarettes, cocaine, and sex. It seems that those neurons make me powerless when tempted by the many delicacies that taste pretty good when crisply fried.

Due to quality standardization and cost control, you'll find in chain restaurants a kitchen designed for frozen portions, fried or microwaved for service. Healthier fresh foods are not their focus, so my best option would be to take refuge in the salads, being careful on my choice of dressing. The pleasure centers in my brain, however, have a preference for hot foods rather than cold ones, so the voices in my head insist on the eggplant Parm.

Though I respect lesser effort, I can't accommodate restaurants' laziness in not cooking from scratch. You don't attain the same results by opening cans and thawing frozen portions. The shortcuts taken by many establishments truly compromise the quality of their products, and at that point, the laziness becomes unacceptable.

I acknowledge that I need to go to a fine dining restaurant for fresher foods, but they have a few inconveniences. Many of the fine restaurants I like require a reservation, which goes against my personal challenges of being organized and punctual in my leisure time. Also, many of the fine restaurants in the area where I live are "bring your own beverage," which requires additional planning. Pennsylvania alcohol laws are very inopportune. I can't buy beer in supermarkets and convenience stores, only at state-licensed stores. These stores don't sell wine. For that, you gotta go to a different, state-owned, shop. As a result, on a Sunday afternoon, on my way to a barbecue and intending to bring a pack of Weissbier to the host, I'm in deep trouble finding booze for sale. The state government extorts as much as $300,000 from an entrepreneur, already overwhelmed by investment costs, willing to attain a liquor license for his or her restaurant, and thus many businesses cannot afford a license to serve a bottle of wine with their entrées. Finally, because I want to try many things at fine restaurants, including mixed drinks, wine, soup, shared appetizer, and dessert, the check is often over a hundred dollars per couple, which isn't an immaterial expense, especially if you like to eat out on a regular basis.

When, however, I break through the sloth and avarice, more often than not I have a good time; so I guess what I need is a little push. For clients like me, who are reluctant to go out to eat, you may need to perform a certain motivational alchemy, turning into gold a combination of two elements: convenience and special interest.

"Convenience," as a general rule, doesn't get me out of my pajamas, but it will make me stop my car on the way back home to buy your food. The idea of convenience includes proximity, price, parking, comfort, and waiting time. I usually categorize fast food, quick service, and chain restaurants in this category. I know exactly what I will get and how much it will cost, usually fitting a smaller budget. I am, however, becoming increasingly reluctant to follow a regimen of empty carbs, sugar, fat, and cholesterol. I would like to live past my fifties.

"Special interest" comprises restaurants that will particularly motivate me to make a reservation, wear shoes instead of sandals, and drive forty-five minutes to enjoy a particular food. The three nearest fine dining vegetarian restaurants in my area are in this category. Blue Sage, Sprig and Vine, and Vedge are excellent restaurants that can make any vegetarian proud to have brought a meat-eater in for a treat, and they are well worth a special effort.

As a business owner, you know whether your place is a convenient neighborhood pizza place or the best artisanal thin-crust pizza in the county. A savvy entrepreneur may even bridge some of the gap between convenience and special interest and tap into the advantages of both worlds. You can't change your location and parking limitations, but you can build an efficient online ordering system and a solid to-go business. Or you may benefit from a convenient location and also step up your quality, to give additional people a reason to take a little detour in their routes to come to your restaurant. Sometimes a Baja Fresh requires a few extra steps than a Qdoba or vice versa, and you want to motivate people to take the extra trouble.

As an owner, you should have a clear vision on what would bring me to your place, other than the fact that your doors are open, for you must have a compelling attractiveness. Do some soul-searching and find what you are or want to be. I presume you did such reflection before you opened, and I believe that revaluating your business plan regularly thereafter will help you keep track of your direction or even change it, if needed. Or it may bring you to an epiphany as to why you don't produce as many sales as you'd like in the location you have. It may be because it's the wrong location for convenience food, or perhaps you're in an area where people are too fast-paced for a fine dining experience. If you are located where most of the population is striving to follow Kashrut dietary laws, your specialization in Southern barbecue pork is probably not appropriate or convenient. You would be surprised how many business owners focus so much on their internal operations that they completely forget the motivations that drive their clients' interests.

I usually have options in my fridge. If I know I'm in for fried frozen portions of bland food, industrial soups, or a lettuce salad, laziness strikes me hard, and I stay home. If I know you have free parking and an excellent grilled Portobello and vegetables sandwich in whole grain ciabatta, I may go get the car keys. If you make an exquisite butternut squash risotto, I'll make reservations.

# Why This Table?

Americans traveling through Europe are often found standing, puzzled, at the entrance of cafés and restaurants, waiting to be greeted and escorted to their tables, while locals just pass by them, sit down at a random table, open a newspaper, light up a cigarette, and wait to be noticed. In most places abroad, you help yourself to the available table of your convenience.

A host, managing reservations and coordinating the seating, is only found when demanded by an extremely busy and often sophisticated establishment.

Personally, I prefer to seat myself. I don't necessarily require a seat by the window with an idyllic view, but rather a discreet table with some privacy and personal space, where I can talk freely, regardless of my chosen topic or use of profane language. I'm the kind of person who likes to make my own decisions, and I feel perfectly capable of choosing the table I want to sit at.

When I come to think about it, being seated by a host doesn't serve my convenience at all. I'm often packed together with busy neighboring tables, while the remainder of the restaurant is empty, as if the heating system's failed and we need to share body heat to keep warm.

So, how are foreigners capable of seating themselves?

- They are used to it. They walk in, choose a table, and sit. Halfway into the restaurant, they may be greeted with a *"Guten tag"* by whichever server first notices them, followed by an array of consonants scratching through the throat, which I assume to mean, "Someone will be with you momentarily."

- European patrons, being economical and low profile in nature, will not choose a six-top table to sit a deuce, so the process is usually efficient and fair. The tables that are reserved have a "Reserved" sign on them, which is usually respected. Anger, when expressed in German, sounds very intimidating, which probably motivates people to be respectful and avoid such confrontation.

- Waiters in Europe are paid a fair salary, and culturally, people there obsess over money less than we do here, so the dispute over better-tipping tables is less savage. Servers are assigned sections, but during a less busy period, they will switch to a sequentially rotating mode, as salespeople do at retail stores. They take turns and respect the rotation, so even if a person sits at the sector assigned to a certain waiter, that client will be attended to by the person whose turn it is. Mutant European servers have developed supernatural memories, and they can recall who attends which table, even when the table is out of their customarily assigned areas.

- Many restaurants split the tips evenly among the servers, as a pool. I presume the waiters there take the slackers and sand-baggers to the back alley at the end of the shift and beat the crap out of them, to sort things out. As a wonderful result, it often doesn't matter which server you wave at to ask for another beer; any server will bring your drink or, at the very least, will pass the message on to the right waiter.

If your restaurant is well-designed and the tables are well-distribut-ed, you are less likely to have a problem with people seating themselves where you don't want them to sit. For example, deuces usually prefer to sit by a wall, instead of in the center of the floor, so make sure to arrange deuce tables alongside the walls instead of only four-top tables and booths. Deuces also like more privacy, so don't place the tables for two among the tables for large groups. If tables are by the door where the freezing wind enters in the winter, or by HVAC vents that blow like a hurricane, no wonder nobody wants to sit there.

As a rule, and with the exception of very busy restaurants with fully booked seating, I have found escorting clients to their tables to be an-other process focused on the restaurant's operational needs, not neces-sarily the client's. The table-escorting service seems to be the tangen-tial spin of a vicious cycle of servers fighting for territory and lack of overall teamwork by the floor staff, associated with clients panicking when left to their own devices. I encourage you to consider question-ing every process you have established for your restaurant; is it focused on the client's enjoyment or only on your operation? This question may drive you to make some changes.

Americans are used to hosts. Depending on your restaurant con-cept, you may be stuck with them, but if you need to trim costs, you could reconsider the necessity of hosts, or maybe your hosts may be able to take additional responsibilities, depending on the time of the day and workload that needs to be dealt with. The cost of the overuse of hosts might eat into the quality of your food or inflate your prices, which isn't good for us clients or for the business. But if you experience periods when your occupancy climbs over 70 percent and you are flipping your tables two or three times per meal rush, then I would agree that you need to organize the table assignments.

Once you determine that you need hosts, make sure you train them and make the most of their role. Hopefully you hired someone who already can smile, so you only need to train them on how to make guests feel warmly welcome, to try to memorize the names of regular clients, and to walk at a reasonable pace, without rushing the arriving clients through the tables, which indicates that they will probably be rushed through the meal. Teach your hosts to offer help to the service staff, to observe the tables as they walk through them, to identify and solve the issues they notice or to advise the service staff of such issues. Show your hosts how to make smart table assignments that address the convenience of your guests.

If you are running lunch with an occupancy of 50 percent, when your lunchtime hostess graduates and resigns, give it a try; have a chat with your waiting staff and see if you can sort out a scheme that allows clients to seat themselves or servers to greet and seat them. My wife will be happy. She wants the window, and it's never offered to her.

# Sahara

Between daydreams in geography class, I'd find myself staring at the map of Africa and realizing the enormity of the Sahara Desert. It makes the majority of the area of ten countries in Northern Africa uninhabitable, because it's that dry and unfertile. The Sahara contributes greatly to the hunger and poverty of the region, but I suppose it also helps to keep apart peoples who would otherwise be killing each other, as happens in more prosperous and populous areas of the same region.

I envisioned this desert with Bedouins under extreme heat, going about their business wearing long robes to protect them from direct sunlight and extreme high temperatures of up to 136°F. The loose robes insulate from the external temperatures and keep sweat from evaporating too quickly. Dehydration from excessive exposure to extreme heat can be deadly. More serious warning symptoms begin with cardiac arrhythmia, organs failure, and unsafe blood pressure changes, to the stage at which you eventually lose consciousness and enter a coma, at which point you would be at the mercy of assistance to stay alive.

I also learned in that class that temperatures drop sharply in the Sahara desert during the night, as low as 5°F. Lack of the tempering humidity you would receive from the sea, lakes, or rivers allows for extreme thermal amplitude within a single day. The nightly cold is another reason the insulation from the wool robes come in handy. When our internal bodily temperature drops below 90 for a prolonged period, the symptoms of hypothermia will start with tachycardia and shivering, a coordinated attempt by the body to produce heat in the muscles closer to the skeleton. Similar to hyperthermia, enduring prolonged periods of low bodily temperature will eventually lead you to lose consciousness and enter into a comatose state. In hyperthermia, prior to your coma, the low oxygenation of your brain causes a state of mental confusion and often giddiness. Not a very disagreeable form of departing this world, but definitely not my cup of tea. I am not a person who likes extreme temperatures, nor am I ready for my afterlife.

Among many other studies of its kind, research conducted in partnership between the Helsinki University of Technology and a division of the U.S. Environmental Protection Agency (EPA), concluded that there is an ideal temperature for human productivity in the work environment. The "perfect" indoor temperature was claimed to be around 70°F. Folks in Finland may be fonder of the cold than my friends in Florida, so depending on local habits and energy costs, you may stretch

that number a few degrees in either direction. I personally start noticing the heat above 78°F and feel cold below 65°F. Most companies
abide by this guideline, and buildings in America will have the HVAC
system set to this range, in which most of us would be comfortable in a
polo shirt or even a jacket and tie.

Here is a caveat, though: if you are responsible for setting the
thermostat of your shop, you ought to take into consideration what I,
the client, will be wearing and how long I will be staying. Here in the
Northeast, the extreme relative heat I feel when I enter a store makes
Christmas shopping that much more unpleasant. In December, I typi-
cally wear a long-sleeved T-shirt, a cotton turtleneck, and a heavy coat,
all of which will keep me comfortable pumping gas into my car while
standing in near-freezing temperatures, but they will make me excru-
ciatingly hot if your heating system is set for 74°F. It's not enough to
open the jacket; I'm rushed to take it off, and it may still be too hot for
my turtleneck. At that point, I will be carrying the coat in my hands,
while I suppose that you, store owner or salesperson, would rather see
me carrying shopping bags.

Give it some thought: look at your demographics and how they
dress, and figure the right temperature for your establishment. Watch
how people behave. Are they removing their clothes? Are they dining
with their coats on? Also bear in mind that older people and women
tend to like it a bit warmer, so take that into consideration, if they are
your typical clients.

Restaurants fit well in the 70°F ideal temperature range, for we
have the habit of removing our jackets before we sit, but if most people
come in turtlenecks and sweaters, tune the dial down a notch. But
don't make it too cold; it will cause the food to cool faster than people
can eat.

There are studies indicating that pushing the temperatures slightly to the colder side could make people slightly uncomfortable, not
enough for it to be unpleasant, but just enough that clients will sub-
consciously eat and leave faster, allowing you to turn more tables. All-
you-can-eat buffets, using this technique of lowering the thermostat,
have reported measurable results that people eat more quickly and less
quantity.

When you set your temperature, make sure you understand that
it's not about your hostess feeling comfortable in her favorite sleeveless shirt, but about me and my turtleneck. If your concern is about
the hostess looking sexier, consider that cooler air may even make the

sleeveless shirt a bit more visually interesting. Colder air may even compel your staff to be more active, so they can keep warm.

Try not to put us through extremes; I chose not to live in the Sahara for a good reason. And if you try to pull the cold-temperature trick on me at your all-you-can-eat buffet, you may get disappointed: I like it colder.

# She Had Me at *Hello*

I was back in my native Rio de Janeiro for Christmas, and I took the opportunity to research the few local vegetarian restaurants. I couldn't avoid noticing that there, as here, vegetarian servers and cooks seem to use a little more cannabis, on average, than their peers in this industry. I don't say this to debate about recreational drugs, the exceptional financial cost that we incur in America by pursuing and incarcerating users of marijuana, or the enormous social cost of drug addiction. I just want to point out that the use of such an herb is not known for making people more efficient. Or more awake. I firmly believe that working intoxicated is a danger for the cooks, significantly counterproductive for the servers, and an overall menace to the quality of your food and service. No matter what you believe, studies have proven that no one performs better at anything after a few puffs. What you do at home after your shift is your problem as long as you show up on time, sober, and looking fresh on the next day. Thankfully, vegetarian clients are significantly more Zen than the average and hardly ever get upset.

The majority of non-ethnic vegetarian restaurants suffer from an exaggerated degree of informality, which doesn't always match well with customary practices of good business management. When a uninitiated client enters a vegetarian restaurant and sees photocopied activist signs Scotch-taped to poorly painted walls, improvised equipment and storage containers, and packs of unlabeled homemade granola for sale around the tables, she may profile the place as not particularly professional. Part of the problem with too much informality is that the setting makes people wonder not so much about the quality of the ingredients, most assumed to be organic, but how they are handled, the sanitation of the kitchen, and the operational status of the refrigeration. This is often an awfully unjust profiling, but a hairy, tattooed, multi-pierced cook in a ragged T-shirt doesn't visually inspire much confidence in kitchen cleanliness.

On the upside, though, the snack bar at a health food store often has a very welcoming aura of relaxation, which can be immensely pleasing and even informative, if you are in such a mood. Chatting to the activist health food store owner could be an edifying experience, as long as you don't sarcastically provoke a discussion by mentioning a news article where you read that a regular apple proved to be just as healthy and nutritious as its organic sibling. You know where the conversation will lead: to a sweating, hyperventilating, red-faced store owner printing dozens of pages from the Internet, showing how the studies sponsored by the agricultural conglomerates are biased and skewed. She will try to save your soul with fervent passion, enumerating every kind of cancer you can get, sooner or later, from the genetically modified vegetables, as well as the pesticides and chemical fertilizers you are ingesting. You may get some amusement from exercising a tree hugger, but for several nights, you'll be thinking of intestinal cancer before you doze, and that can ruin a good night's sleep.

The first vegetarian restaurant I went to in Rio was like that, but instead of granola, they sold packs of organic whole grain rice. As I walked in, I saw a menu board written with chalk, memorized a couple of things that caught my attention, and seated myself. The place seated some forty people and was full. The three servers were busy, but not overwhelmed. The lunch combos only had five options, so taking the order was not particularly difficult. I decided not to call a server, intentionally seeing how long it would take them to realize I wasn't being attended. After some twenty minutes, my wife lost interest in my experiment and started to wave. Promptly, a cute young woman who had passed by our table 178 times stopped, explained the dishes, took our order, and returned with the starter salads with no further delay. It was great! Except for the fact that nobody had ever checked if we were being attended for the previous third of an hour. Maybe they were doing their own experiment to check how long it would take us to start waving for service. We had been rather confused from the moment we entered the restaurant, wondering if we had to order at the cashier or directly to someone in the open kitchen. My strategy of giving time to the servers to get ready for us had clearly been a mistake, and who knows how much longer it would have taken for the server to ask if we were ready to order.

The second vegetarian restaurant was a bit more awkward. We entered, seated ourselves, and waited for a server. There were two servers in the house and a cashier, who was having a happy conversation with his girlfriend over the restaurant's phone. Only three tables were occupied. The servers ignored us, and we couldn't make eye contact with them for some ten minutes. Before my wife waved her hand, I stood up and checked around the place. At an extension to the adjacent dining room, there was a buffet, which we couldn't see from the entrance or from where we sat. The servers probably guessed that if we weren't getting food, we were waiting for additional people to arrive and join us, so they chose to give us privacy and never bothered us by offering anything. At both places, the food was good, not spectacular, but savory and fairly priced, so I was still happy.

The third restaurant had disappeared. We went to the address informed on the website and found the property empty. A neighbor guessed that they moved to the opposite side of town, but wasn't sure. A trip almost wasted, but for a beautiful nearby museum we wanted to visit anyway.

The fourth was still there, but being renovated. I hope they had a good reason for the strange timing for the construction, because no sane mind would decide to renovate a restaurant during the Christmas and New Year holidays, the busiest time of the year for tourism, shopping, and dining out in the city. Another disappointing trip.

The fifth (and last) restaurant was open. The small buffet had seating for thirty people. We walked in at 3:00 p.m., so the dining room only contained us and another fella. "Hello," a woman said from the counter as we entered. "If this is your first time here, we serve this all-you-can-eat buffet. Please feel free to help yourselves when you are ready or, if you'd like, we have a few items *a la carte*." She offered iced tea and smoothies for drinks, letting us know that the complete drinks list was on the menu over at our table, recommending the pineapple and mint juice as being very popular. "I'll be right with you," she concluded. She finished quickly with the paperwork she was working on and took our smoothie orders. We liked the buffet option, since we had been hungry for a couple of hours then, but above all, we were happy to find a vegetarian place run and attended by normal people. The food was good, but she had already totally had us at hello.

Moral of the story: the food wasn't significantly better in any of the places, nor was any place fancier or particularly well decorated. The last place was organized mildly better, but it was the immediate attention we received that gave us that sense of order. Our perception of that restaurant's professionalism instantaneously improved, and I'd bet that a focus group would have responded that that restaurant looked much neater and cleaner than the previous ones, even if it weren't necessarily so.

In case you're wondering, I'm not looking for the feel of an automated mass-production kind of professional food place. I love mom-and-pop restaurants and the warm personal attention that is characteristic of them. I'm just looking for an orderliness that assures me that things are well cared for. If the service is apathetic and confused, it makes me uneasy, as if my eyes catch the operator of a carnival roller coaster napping while I'm spinning.

The "Hello" woman was awake.

# Latino Telemarketers

I've clearly made it to a database of Spanish speakers, and I receive many telemarketing calls in *español* at home. They don't seem to bother with the national "Do not call" list, and I'm doomed to be targeted with sales of English classes, international dialing cards, and special banking services.

If you've worked with a Latino, you probably noticed that we are quite longwinded. Spanish telemarketing calls go like this: "Good evening, do I have the pleasure to be speaking with Mr. Peralta? Do you speak Spanish, Mr. Peralta? Well, very good evening, Mr. Peralta, my name is Maria Consuelo Alfonso Avila de la Cruz, how are you this wonderful evening? I'm delighted to hear that you are well. We are, at this time, contacting Spanish speakers all across America to inform them of a very special opportunity..." *Click.* I'm sorry. I will allow about ten seconds for you to introduce the topic, else I will hang up. I may also hang up after you introduced the topic, but at least you'd have had a chance to catch my interest. Latino callers waste it all in greetings. I know it's rude, but since telemarketers are trained to speak uninterrupted, the only choice I'm left with is to hang up. On a few occasions I waited for my opportunity to explain to the caller that I was not interested, but as a word of advice, I would encourage them to get to the point just a bit more quickly, that I would at least get to know what the offer was about. My Colombian wife—used to conversational rituals with interminable exchanges of "how are you," "how have you been," "what's up," and "how's it going"—tells me that my impatience is abnormal, and she doesn't mind the introductory courtesies at all.

In some restaurants the host or the waiter will ask, "Have you dined with us before?" to which I invariably and promptly reply *yes*, regardless of whether I have or have not been there before. Unfortunately, there's always someone innocent or honest at the table who will unadvisedly answer a sincere *no*, which will prompt the host or waiter to discourse about the history of the establishment and their philosophical approach to food and hospitality, how the founder rose from a childhood of deprivation in Chicago to build a food empire, all due to a secret tomato sauce recipe his grandmother whispered in Toni's ear at her deathbed. Seriously, guys, you are a chain Italian restaurant, not the Coliseum. There is an overwhelming probability that you don't have a history that I would care to listen to. Please stop right there. I don't have the least bit of interest. If I did want to know more about the restaurant, as I oftentimes do, I'm sure you will have a friendly and resourceful website. Let me research on my own; if I have questions, I'll bring them with me next time.

Also, I'm not good at all with names. I never address by name an acquaintance that I bump into at a movie theater. It's too risky. It's hard for me when the person is out of context; at work I know his name, but at the Regal Cineplex, I can't connect the right string of neurons. I take no risks and instead say, "Hey, man, how are you? How's everybody doing?" Then I hope for an answer that will help me recall who this person and "everybody" are. I'm good with faces; I know this guy. I also know that he's very nice, but even if I remember where I know him from, names are tough for me. I'm just like my mother, who, when addressing me, goes through all my brothers' names until she finally gets to mine.

It makes me feel bad when Brad tells me he will be my server for that night, because I will immediately forget that his name is Brad. I don't mean to dehumanize Brad, but I'm not sure it's really important for our relationship that evening that he introduces me to his name. I was told that a server introducing herself by name is a better fit culturally in the South and on the West Coast than in the Northeast. I'm not sure how it might have started. It could possibly have been that Jane wanted Coppola and Scorsese, habitual diners at the restaurant, to remember her name for their next movies. It could just be that Jane wanted to be perceived as an individual, a unique entity full of life, love, and dreams. I also read in an article that introducing yourself by your name is one of fifty things supposed to help servers get better gratuities according to servers' street wisdom. I found the other forty-nine tip-enhancing suggestions to sound more promising: from actually being a competent server to dressing a bit sexy without looking vulgar. I also read that this self-introduction is a big no-no in New York, where you can be physically assaulted for wasting people's time with chitchat. For me, I believe not exchanging personal information would better preserve the magic of the beautiful moment spent together.

When I arrived here in America, I found it a bit unusual that servers were introducing themselves to me with their names; nowhere else had I seen that practice before. For a moment I even thought they were all, guys and girls, hitting on me, and it bumped up my self-esteem. In my hometown, knowing the waiter's name was a privilege of habitual clients. In exchange, the server would know your drinking and eating preferences, which was a way of impressing your date for the evening.

A good guideline for servers is to act naturally. Remember the story about how you should serve from the left and collect from the right? If you are useless with your left hand, what the hell, man, serve from the right. It's much better than dropping the sauce or messing up the plate presentation as you lay it on the table. Practice at home and bring it on when you are proficient and it looks natural.

The self-presentation doesn't actually bother me, I just find it unnecessary. I would suggest that you do it if it truly feels natural to you. If you enjoy introducing yourself by name, it will sound natural and pleasing and you will make a good connection with the client. If you feel obligated to introduce yourself like an automated voice system, it won't work. Don't do it because you believe it's a rule of good service conduct, one of the things a server must do. It isn't. It may be a rule of the restaurant you work for, in which case, if you want to keep your job, you should respect their policy.

As an alternative, if Brad wears his nametag on the uniform, I may be compelled to call him by his name, even if he didn't introduce himself. When I see him, I can take a quick Humphrey Bogart glance at his embroidery and say, "Hello, Brad, how are you tonight?" Then I can ask him to bring me "the usual." It will mess him up, because I don't have a usual, but it will certainly impress my friends.

On the other hand, it is opportune for Brad to learn my name if I frequent his restaurant. Calling clients by their names is a classical good practice that is usually very well perceived and makes people feel welcome. After handling my credit card a few times, Brad may be able to learn my name without too much trouble, if he is paying attention. Most clients are likely to reciprocate by learning Brad's name as well.

Overall, I recommend avoiding too much chatter. I've seen clients who do enjoy long talks with servers, while other people use their mealtime to catch up with their friends and may dislike having their conversations at the table being intruded or interrupted too often or for too long. As a rule for professional situations, you should err on the side of being discreet and objective.

# Can I Help You?

I don't go to McDonald's very often, nor Burger King, Pizza Hut, or the many other fast food restaurants. In addition to my health concerns about a diet based on saturated and animal fats combined with refined carbohydrates of little nutritional value, I've had cafeterias in all buildings where I worked and, although the food was generally short of being great, it was more convenient than going out for fast food, and the cafeterias offered choices that were less detrimental to my health. Don't get me wrong, I do enjoy an occasional BK Veggie or a vegetarian Taco Bell burrito and, before opting for being vegetarian, I would have a Whopper or Big Mac every now and then. I am not completely hypocritical. I understand many fast foods taste good. I'm just vigilant to make sure my diet is varied, and I push to make it healthier.

Since I go sporadically, I have a curiosity for the novelties on the menu, like the McRib, which is now back and will be gone again by the time this book reaches your hands. I'm usually also scanning in hope for a new vegetarian option.

It bothers me quite a bit that, as soon I start to look at the menu display, the cashier will ask, "Can I help you?" Why? Set aside the bad semantic construction; what good purpose could possibly come from this question? I am obviously reading the menu board, squinting, since the fonts get tinier every day, for all the space is taken by the photos of combos one through eight. Now I gotta stop reading, face the attendant, answer, and find where I had stopped.

If you are wondering, no, I'm not standing in line; I am as far from the counter as my eyesight can manage, and my body language doesn't indicate in any manner that I want help. Of course, instead of replying, "For the love of Pete, man, can't you see I'm reading the menu?" I just say, "No, thank you; I just need a moment." But I would prefer you to allow me to seek help at my own pace and time; otherwise I just feel that you are rushing me.

You are doing me no favors by vaguely offering help at an inopportune time. If I'm reading the menu, what help could I possibly need? If I had a question, I would ask, but I suppose I can figure out the difference between a single, double, or triple burger. Don't do this anymore, please. You don't have to show me that you are a devoted employee this way. When I walk toward your cash register, and you greet me with a smile, I will know how nicely attentive you are. The whole "Can I help you?" thing really, really pisses me off; it's useless and distracting. Please stop.

It happens in retail, too. Like many, I enjoy browsing novelties in Best Buy. They ran customer satisfaction surveys and received some bad feedback on customer service, so now they flood their stores with temporary staff during holiday shopping season and, no matter how good a dribbler you are, you can't cross the store without being asked five times, "Can I help you?" There, the issue is that they have, consistently, proven to be incapable of actually helping me. Try asking a temp worker to help you with the choice between a plasma and an LCD TV which are priced equally. "Well, sir, one is plasma and the other is LCD." Well, they are both good brands, and from what I can see here, the picture looks about the same… "Sir, they are both good TVs. It's a matter of preference." Possibly, I think, but something has to be different: color performance, black resolution, functionalities, consumer problems, and returns. How many HDMI ports does it have? Does it have a port for a VGA cable out of my PC? They never know, ever. So they start reading the tag for me. Sorry, mate, but I don't need a buddy for reading the tags; I can do that on my own. If you can't bring any expertise to the conversation, I'd rather you not offer help.

I know this sounds mean. I'm not such a horrible person, but I detest being interrupted for a conversation doomed to go nowhere. All I want is for you to let me make the decision of when I want to ask for help, just like I would like to be able to sneeze and be left alone without receiving a shower of blessings.

Unfortunately, when I do decide to seek help to unlock a cage and fetch me a GPS, I can't find anyone available. An older gentleman is to be found trying to figure out the technology of a digital camera, and I will then have to wait awhile until I can talk to the salesman, or whatever they call their salesmen at Best Buy.

Another frustration happens at Home Depot and Lowe's, also frequent stops for me. They must have read the same customer service survey, and now they also approach me frequently throughout the aisles, offering help. Most of those guys, at least at the stores close to my house, are very good. They know their stuff: where things are, how to use them, and why the last thing I tried didn't work. Often at HD and Lowe's, I don't know how to phrase my questions or the name of any item I'm looking for. Most of the time, I don't even know if what I'm looking for exists: I'm looking for a thing that will prevent my bike rack from scratching the paint on the tailgate door, or something to keep a bird out of my dryer's exhaust vent. Or I go to the store to figure out the pipes and connectors I need to replace my kitchen sink with a double sink, and I haven't actually inspected or measured anything on the existing connection. I could actually use some help, but the interaction is enormously frustrating.

—Can I help you, sir?

—Well, maybe. I'm installing a kitchen sink. My previous sink had a single thing, and now I bought one with a double thing, so I'm looking for a thing to connect two pipes to the floor drain, but one side of the sink has a disposal, and the height is very different from where I need to connect the other side.

—Oh, I see; you need a bi-fold zapontric connector, a raccaska extension, and a cobrisca dillector to center your drain. Is the caffofle of the redocter attached to the drainpipe or to the sink pipe?

—I don't know.

—In most houses it's attached to the drain. Is your pipe two and a quarter inches or two and five-eighths?

—Not sure; you see, I'm metric. Aren't those things standard?

—Not if your house is over twenty years old.

—Does it matter?

—The caffofle won't fit the redocter; it will be too large.

—Ah, that is not a problem at all... When that happens, I just put a bunch of that white plumbing tape, and it works fine.

—Sir, you should consider calling a professional plumber.

In that case, it's me. I can't express myself in the language of professional plumbing. The conversation takes forever, and I end up entirely humiliated and have to listen to my wife saying: "Did you hear what he said? I told you should call a plumber; you'll flood the basement again." As if the past two times the leaks had been my fault or as if I needed the words of advice—also known as discouragement—wives offer so well. Pardon my stubbornness, but I prefer to search for things on my own. After a few frustrated evenings, merchandise exchanges, a furious wife, and many rolls of plumbing tape, the new sink works like a charm.

Lowe's and Home Depot may better improve the customer service surveys by assigning more people to the kitchen design desk, the key copying desk, the blinds cutting desk, the lumber cutting desk, and all such stations where help is needed, but hardly ever found.

If you spot my indecisiveness and genuinely want to interact while I'm reading the menu, be specific: instead of "May I help you?" how about "Would you like to try our new Tennessee barbecue chickpea veggie burger? It's $6.75." It will be more productive for all of us.

Unfortunately for me, although I'd rather shop on my own, retail studies prove sales increase by directing your client to special deals or simply offering: "May I help you find anything in the store?" I suggest, though, that you look for body language: if I am desperately walking away from you and purposely avoiding eye contact, you may want to give me a moment before engaging me in conversation.

# Personal Space

The anthropologist Edward Hall spent decades studying behavioral differences among human cultures, from the American indigenous tribes in New Mexico to the different ethnicities in the Philippines. One particular aspect of interest for Dr. Hall was the dimension of space in non-verbal communication. We are now very familiar with this concept, but the study was quite revolutionary for the day.

He concluded that the use of space is an important form of personal expression and that culture influences the amount of surrounding space that individuals perceive to be personal. The distance that people establish while having a conversation is itself a form of communication, and the dynamics in managing such distance can determine the outcome of the interaction. In case you doubt that anthropology is a practical science, let's look at a real-life scenario: let's say that you're interested in someone, but you aren't quite sure if your feelings are reciprocated. At a suitable venue, you can test the person's comfort level with your physical proximity in a conversation, as a good indicator as to if you will get lucky. As long as he seems comfortable, continue the conversation while getting closer by gradual, almost unnoticeable, increments of a quarter-inch. Once very close, try to casually lay your hand over his arm, then over his knee. If there are no signs of discomfort, your chances are excellent.

I can attest to the discomfort of arriving in Delhi and adapting to the extreme proximity offered at all times by large masses of people. Or the contrast between South America, where people keep a closer distance and touch each other frequently during a conversation, and puritan and aloof Pennsylvania. After having lived here in Pennsylvania for a few years, I had a work colleague who stood frighteningly close to me every time we needed to talk. He talked loudly, too. He naturally did that to everybody. I found it agonizing. I could barely pay attention to the conversation, usually work-related, and all I could think about was a strategy to escape that unpleasant closeness.

Dr. Hall advised on the importance of understanding personal space in different cultures to attain better success in diplomacy and business negotiations between people of different countries, in a world that, in the 1960s, was still far from globalization.

If you know people from South America and Europe, you may have noticed that when a man and a woman meet, they greet each other with a kiss or two on the cheek. Women greet each other in the same manner and, though less frequently, two men may do the same. Sometimes, to protect the makeup, women do the air kiss or bump their head against your temporal bone, in a practice that poses serious risks of long-term concussion.

If you are American, you may have been surprised when you offered a foreigner a kiss-less hug and received a kiss on your cheek. Or when another foreigner sat a little too close beside you on a public bench. At the time of the study, in the fifties and sixties, Americans liked to enjoy some eighteen inches of inviolable personal space. Not much has changed, but metropolitan habitants have adapted to be a little cozier with each other.

I enjoy having a lot of personal space. Unless I know you very well, I behave like my cat: I like being around, but don't get too close to me or I may scratch or hide under the table. Because of my obsession with personal space, I have a preference that differs significantly from what you may have learned in hospitality school: I don't like you constantly filling my wine glass. I would much rather you leave the wine bottle on the table and don't mess with it. Every time you approach the table, you are invading my personal space and disrupting the conversation.

The habit of waiters filling the glasses comes from a time where servers were actually servants and were to be ignored and deemed invisible. If you approach my table today, I will acknowledge, greet you, and thank you every single time, but you just interrupted the conversation. Now I can't remember what I was talking about. Ah, yes, the glasses... Sorry, restaurant critics and French instructors of hospitality, but I respectfully believe the practice of filling wine glasses is dated.

For the water, I recommend that you use slightly bigger glasses, which require fewer refills, especially if your menu has a lot of hot chilies, salt, or soy sauce. If the table is large enough, leave a carafe of ice water on it.

It's not that I don't like you being close. According to Dr. Hall, the major issue is that I don't know you too well yet, and I need to build a relationship with you to feel comfortable with your presence in my personal space. I would ask you to please try to minimize this intrusion while I make acquaintance with you. It keeps you safe, too... If you get too close, who knows, I may kiss you on the cheek.

# Advertising

My dad was a partner at a small advertising agency back in his day. I was young, but interested enough to listen to his adult colleagues when they conversed. One thing I learned is that folks in the Creative Department are not the most business-oriented, often more focused on exercising creativity. I also learned that such people tend to have enlarged egos and adore winning prizes.

The bad news for those hiring an advertising agency is that a genially created, beautifully executed, and award-winning advertising campaign doesn't necessarily sell your product.

You may laugh your lungs out during an ad that cost several millions for a single air spot on Super Bowl Sunday, but it may neither significantly raise awareness of a particular brand, nor make clients more willing to buy it. In many cases, a few seconds later we may have completely forgotten the brand of laundry detergent featured in the commercial we just watched, despite its portrayal of the most beautiful infant cherubim dressed in the purest shade of white.

I, for one, being a political news junkie, often have CNN on while doing other things, like writing this book. I find CNN reporting a touch less biased than Fox News and MSNBC, but, of course, all the analysis, done by professional partisan pundits, is equally biased. While CNN is on, I rarely look at the screen. Many of the commercials on CNN do not voice the product's name, so I end up hearing a number of ads, some of which I even memorize, but I haven't a clue of what product the ad sells or what the brand is. I wonder if the creators of those pieces won prizes for them. I also wonder how many people, like me, don't keep their eyes on the screen during commercials.

If you are an independent restaurant owner, you probably can't afford much advertising; certainly not on prime time TV. Maybe you choose radio spots, between one car dealer sale and another, the ones with recorded men (always men) yelling about the lowest prices ever, sounding like, well, salesmen, and we all know how much we like to listen to salesmen yelling. Maybe your ad is an oasis of peaceful sound between the men shouting: "Joe went crazy, every car must go, hyper-mega blowout sales event this Saturday only; limited to only one car per person, please." If you match the right programming and demographic to your restaurant style, I'm told that radio advertising works well. Just make sure that your restaurant's name gets highlighted in the piece. Not the joke or the music, these are just the accessories to promote your brand (restaurant).

If you do advertise, please don't lie. An ice cream company recently took a hard hit to their reputation when they were ordered by court to remove the "all natural" label from their package. It seems that the emulsifiers, sweeteners, stabilizers, and flavoring additives are not quite found in nature, requiring significant chemical manipulation before making it into your frozen delicacy. Honest mistake, they claimed.

Stay on message. The most disagreeable man I ever met was also quite smart and had a simple rule: make sure your message tells what the product is, what it does, and why it is better than the competition's. If you make that clear and pleasant to listen to, you'll hit the advertising jackpot.

# Internet

Early in the '90s, this new venue for communication arose, proliferating chain letters of bad jokes, photos of cute animals, and requests for help from alleged heirs of African dictators in assisting to transfer funds of their inherited fortune in exchange for a cut of their wealth. In those days, I worked for a technology firm and remember many discussions on how to make money out of something that was born free, other than for the connection services fee. Once the tremendous business potential of this new medium was globally acknowledged, millions of people, by entrepreneurship or stock investment, quickly jumped in. On one hand, this created the spectacular distortions where virtual companies like etoys.com attained a market capitalization significantly higher than well-established companies such as Toys "R" Us and KB Toys, while on the other hand, newly-founded empires like Yahoo and Google solidified themselves among the greatest companies in the world.

The misunderstanding of the success factors by some newborn companies was proportionate to the misunderstanding of the role the Internet would take in our society. We now better understand the Internet as an enabler, rather than as an end in itself. Founding a dotcom capable of potentially reaching billions of people is meaningless if such enterprise doesn't provide any meaningful service or cannot deliver what it proposes to deliver. Exposure is as valuable as content.

I now depend on the Web for my news, shopping, food, and restaurant research, and many other mundane activities, such as looking up movie times and booking tee times at my neighborhood golf course. I have a VoIP phone service, use Skype for international calls, and am constantly checking my e-mail on my Android phone.

If you own a restaurant, unless you are in an Amish village, you must have a website. You probably already do. Allow me, please, to suggest some *dos* and *don'ts* for your Internet presence.

**Front Page:** Keep it simple. Don't overpopulate with data, Flash, and animation, because it makes the page difficult to read, and it will run very slowly on some devices. Your page must contain your full address, including ZIP code, so I can map it in Google or my GPS. You must also display your current hours of operation and provide a contact phone number—assuming you'll answer it; otherwise, don't include the number. Absolutely do not include music or sounds, because in addition to further slowing down my computer, it reveals to our co-workers that we are not exactly working, at that moment.

You should have a neat, easy-to-navigate menu bar linking to your secondary pages. You may want to add a few photos that convey the essence of your restaurant, including the dining room ambience and the food. You should invest in a good photographer and a food designer to make the best of what you have; the photos are important. You don't want your dishes to look pale, greasy, or with food piled up like it was served in the army canteen.

**Reservations:** I will personally be pleased if you offer online reservations. I'm a bit reluctant to spend time on the phone and prefer to make reservations online whenever possible. If you do offer online reservations, don't do what my car maintenance shop does. I fill in an online service request on a form that includes desired date and time, as well as the nature of the service. They then call me back to confirm the whole thing, so I end up giving every piece of information twice. If I wanted to talk on the phone, I would have called to begin with! A few Internet service companies outsource online reservations services, and that seems to work very well. You provide the design of your restaurant and seating availability, and they process the reservations for you. Keep up with technological developments in social media that may bring further convenience in communications between clients and between these clients and your restaurant for dining arrangements. Most likely, the transactional capabilities in Twitter and Facebook will eventually allow setting a reservations system in that type of platform.

**Photos:** Resist the temptation of making sure that you or your lovely wife, your mother-in-law, and other family members to whom you owe investment money appear on the photos. Maybe your sister has just had a silicone job done and now wants to show everybody how firm they look in a tight shirt, but the photos are not about egos, they're about the food and ambience of your restaurant. It's OK to show the chef holding a flaming sauté pan and an elegant server in the dining room, but unless you run a strip bar, keep it professional. Make sure to keep the lighting appropriate and the colors well-represented in digital media.

I have browsed a few books by food designers, and I educated myself on the importance of their work. Even simple food can look well-structured, neatly presented, and appealing. It's your image being presented to the world; it must be at its Sunday best. Equally important, make sure that the photos display the same food that you actually serve. Too many times I feel that I went to an entirely different restaurant from the one I saw in the pictures.

**Menu:** Of course, if I'm browsing your restaurant website, I want to see what you serve and the prices, but here you have the opportunity to be a bit more extensive about the ingredients and preparation, since there's no server waiting for my decision. You may want to highlight the quality of your cheeses, the local sourcing of your produce, and the health benefits of the ingredients and cooking methods. I've seen a website that does a very good job in disclosing ingredients for people who have specific concerns due to food allergies or intolerances.

**About Us:** Here you show who you are and why you are in the business. Tell me about your experience, inspiration, and philosophy. "We serve quality food fast," "We want to promote the joy of a relaxed dinner," "We prepare the authentic offal stew from West Uzbekistan," etc. Tell us how long you have been in business and your involvement in the community. Overall, I'm not interested in your religious orientation or your position on abortion, but if you really want to limit your clientele, go ahead and participate in some activism.

**Green:** It will benefit you to highlight specific environmental initiatives, such as recycling, the use of energy-efficient equipment, and other conscientious environmental behavior, like fair-trade international sources for your ingredients. Folks from the Green Restaurant Association, a reputable organization that audits and certifies restaurant "greenness," attest very good results in free marketing and client response for green initiatives.

**The Chef:** If you have a steady lead chef, as opposed to cooks who don't last much more than a couple of months, a lot of people would like to know about her, now that a lot of chefs are viewed as celebrities. This will make your restaurant look more distinguished.

**Press:** If you have had good press and received awards, you certainly want to post them on your website. Check with your lawyer to see if you can use photos of celebrities who ate at your restaurant, or contact the celebrities' PR for authorization. Endorsement is a powerful tool to strengthen your credibility.

**Newsletters:** Ten times out of ten, when I have subscribed to a website's newsletter, I later regretted it bitterly. The overwhelming majority of newsletters are, well, overwhelmingly too frequent and entirely useless. I get newsletters from my development's association, the energy company, the water company, the insurance company, the township, the school district, dozens of chain stores and online retailers, the local community college, my car manufacturer, car dealers, local churches, etc. I don't read any of them anymore. They all go to the spam folder.

It's a complete waste of e-mail or printed paper. If you want to use a newsletter, make sure to send it very seldom, in most cases no more than four times a year, and only if you have something to say: new operating hours (like "now open for lunch") or a new seasonal menu. Be concise, and maybe add a good recipe or a cooking trick, to compel me to keep your letter.

**Contact E-mail:** Why offer a contact e-mail if you won't read them? If you have an e-mail address on your website, make sure you respond with a personalized—not automated—message. E-mails can be useful for collecting feedback on your menu and service, and possibly for adjusting your recipes and identifying opportunities for training your staff.

**Suppliers:** In a recent survey by the National Restaurant Association, the number one trend pointed out by chefs was local sourcing of produce and meats. If you work with local farms, you may want to highlight this fact and even name some of your local purveyors, as long as they are not involved with any recent food-poisoning scandals. If you are loyal to a particular high-end brand or product, or if you go out of your way to offer special vegan wines, organic eggs, or Himalayan rice that is not related to child slavery, you may want to disclose that, too.

**Blogs:** I am not a blogger—at least not yet—but I occasionally visit blogs looking for specific information: "How do I replace the broken screen on my cell phone?" "How do I fix car dents?" "How to make vegan Hollandaise?" "How good is the XYZ road bicycle?" What I usually find is a bizarre array of silliness. Why do people take the time to post responses on something about which they are noticeably clueless? And why would anyone log on to a blog, read a string of messages, and post, "I don't know how to do this either. I hope someone does." It is insane! When you actually find information on the top ten smart phones, top ten culinary schools, etc., it's usually a composition of opinionated statements backed by no facts or reasoning. "My friend Jen went to Johnson & Wales, and she thought it was great, definitely one of the best."

So, how about a blog on your restaurant's website? Don't do it. You won't have the time to participate in the conversations, and you won't be able to control the propriety of the conversations. I am all for the First Amendment of our Constitution, but some concepts I wouldn't want to support or promote on my restaurant's website, and some conversational content I wouldn't find appropriate.

If you would like to promote your restaurant through blogs, find an appropriate website with groups of food enthusiasts, and comment there. Be honest about who you are. If you are a restaurant owner, introduce yourself as such, instead of, "Hey, my name is John. You gotta check out this new restaurant that just opened!" You will eventually be caught, and it will harm your credibility. Engaging on forums with enthusiasts may not only help divulge your brand, but also bring you good feedback about your food and service.

These days, websites and blogs must harmonize with social media venues, like Facebook and Twitter. Your website works fine for static information, but you would need to send out a tweet to let people know your soup of the day or the evening's specials. Use the same good reasoning you'd use with any other media. Tweet only when you have something to say, and not too often, or you will be unfriended.

# I Can't Follow Directions

"Oh, I believe it's by that old brick building at Wood and Eleventh. Pretty sure. The one with a red door, I think. I had a buddy that lived around there. Kind of rough there. Why would you want to go there anyway? Anyhow, man, you may want to continue here on Green Street. You would think you can go down Wood here on Seventeenth, but the traffic on Wood goes west until you get to Broad. But don't try to go south on Broad. There's construction on the corner with Spring Garden, and the whole thing is a nightmare. Apparently there was some gas leakage or whatnot, so if I were you, I would go all the way here on Green until Twelfth and make a right, and it will take you to Wood, but good luck finding parking there; it's all private lots and they're always towing people there. You might as well just want to start looking for parking around here."

People may think I'm one of those guys who won't ask for directions just out of pure macho pride. Indeed, I hate asking for directions, but it's simply out of embarrassment of my short span of attention, which probably matches that of a four-year-old.

Those who know me a bit will understand my frenetic nodding, accompanied by "right," "OK, make a left," "hmm hmm," "third traffic light," and "got it." Well, I didn't get it. You lost me on the second turn. From then on it was just noise, like the mumbling sound when the teacher is talking to Charlie Brown.

All evidence might suggest the contrary—wandering eyes, driving in circles, and many curse words—but I know exactly where I am and how to get to where I want to go. We'll get there, just a few moments late. Fashionably late. To my despair, my wife winds down the window and starts asking people for directions, just to later be upset that I didn't pay attention to what they said.

Sometimes restaurants have a list of "Today's specials" that is longer than most Easter Sunday sermons. I can't follow it. The waiter will pull off a card and recite, in monotone, a listing of appetizers and soups and meats and fish and pasta and salads, to which I nod with increasing vigor, hoping that, like Jeannie or Samantha (ask your parents, they know), the nod will make that agonizing moment go away. It's painful. I might have retained the words "root vegetables," but I certainly don't remember how they are prepared or what else is on the plate. Asking the waiter to repeat is like saying, "Sorry, sir, when you stepped on my toes, you didn't catch all five of them. Would you please do it again?" Since I don't really enjoy pain, I revert back to the comfort of the menu, where I can understand the dishes at my own slow pace.

I have rarely, if ever at all, seen any special entrée that is vegetarian, and that factor definitely drives me to not pay attention to the list of specials for the day.

I'm also a paranoid Trekkie, convinced that rebellious Klingons are out there to get me. I happen to know that everything in the walk-in refrigerator is perishable or has a use-by date, so I can't avoid being slightly suspicious of specials. This concern is often unfounded, for specials are also an opportunity for chefs to exercise their creativity and test new ideas that could potentially refresh the permanent menu. Some restaurants use the specials wisely to serve seasonal produce when these items can be found locally at their best flavor, without the need to be transported around the world, overusing energy resources and contributing to increasing global warmth.

A few ideas to soften people like me:

- Keep the specials to two or three items at most and, preferably, give me a printed list of the daily specials. If the chef's creative impetus cannot be contained and the list of specials is almost as long as the regular menu, then you certainly must print it and attach it to the menu. The waiter is welcome to refer to them, read them up for us if he will, but I would be able to refresh my memory with a nice piece of printed paper.

- Tell me a story: "We are in the peak of the tomato season. We received a load of spectacular organic heirloom tomatoes from our local farmers, and everything with tomatoes on the menu is at its best. Today, the chef prepared a Caprese salad with fresh buffalo mozzarella, reduced Italian balsamic, fresh basil, roasted pistachios, and lemon zest that is out of this world. I strongly recommend it."

- Spend some time with the chef understanding the preparation and ingredients of the special. Hopefully the chef will prepare plates for the floor staff to taste the specials, which will make it much easier for the servers to describe the dish, rather than simply read from a notepad.

- If the list of specials is large and cannot be attached to the menu, you'll have to summarize and omit details of ingredients and preparation and just refer to "Seasonal Tomatoes Caprese" and use buzz words that I will catch: lasagna, smoked tofu, zucchini blossom, etc.

When reciting the specials, you will face another critical issue: the decision of whether or not to disclose the specials' prices. Many restaurants choose not to list the prices—something that always bothers me and really pisses off Penny, a close friend who is a smart and conscious shopper—or end the beautiful description of your plate with the anti-climax of declaring its value, which my wife hates. When you print the specials and attach it to the menu, the problem is solved.

# Language

In one of my most recent corporate roles, I had more contact with clients than I had in previous internal functions. To my astonishment, I found that clients were fluent in our own internal verbiage, for they found it the only effective means of communicating with us. I felt embarrassed. No client should be forced to learn our crazy language to navigate our bureaucracy. I've come across much jargon and scrambled letters in every company I worked for. They serve a twofold purpose: they facilitate communication, giving specifics on the product, department, report, or process you are referring to, and they afford the old-timers a sense of superiority, as the perplexed newcomers are left helplessly disoriented throughout the meeting—assuming they could find the meeting room MSB-2 West.

The restaurant world has its own jargon for processes, ingredients, and cooking methods. Until recently, I had no idea what they meant. Nor should I. Why would I know the anecdote about Delmonico's Steak being item number 86, and that it was so popular, the kitchen often ran out of it before the night was over? This is the kind of lore that helps identify who's familiar with the trade and who's a novice, like checking for hair on the arms of a grill cook.

You may want to take a look at your menu and ensure that it's intelligible to the uninitiated. Or did you intentionally want it to be unintelligible to attain an aura of sophistication?

Look for words like *farci*, braise, *coulis*, *quenelle*, and *fumet*. I assure you that most clients don't know what those are. The sous chef at a restaurant where I worked was convinced that we didn't sell much of the Vichyssoise soup or dishes containing quinoa, farro, and escarole, because many people simply didn't know what they were and were too embarrassed to ask. I believe the sous chef was absolutely correct. Follow "Swiss chard" by the words "dark greens," and confused clients are now back in the conversation.

A few weeks ago at a Japanese restaurant, the waiter offered us wonderful "ten-size" scallops. It was only when I entered the restaurant world that I learned that the reference is a size measurement, indicating that there would be ten scallops per pound. Pretty big fellas, considering the average size of scallops is around twenty per pound. But, who really knows that? Nor did I know that EVOO (often on menus) stands for extra virgin olive oil, that offal meats are entrails like kidney and tripe, and that *aioli* is a garlic mayo. If you must say that your chicken was braised, then say it was braised in a lemongrass and green curry sauce, and I will figure out that you cooked it in a liquid.

As you check your menu, also make sure the descriptions of your dishes mean something. There seems to have been a bad batch of marketing advice on plate descriptions that resulted in meaningless expressions like "explosion of oriental flavors," "blast of spices," "discharge of juices," "effusion of elements," and other pyromaniac bullshit of that sort, which doesn't help me in any capacity to better understand the options and make my choice.

Your menu should also be free of anything that would make you look foolish or offend a community. A restaurant famously achieved both these feats by listing on the menu a dish of "Crab Cakes made from Alaskan King Crabs from Maine."

As a rule, keep your dish names and descriptions concise; convey the main ingredients and preparation method, but without too much fluff. We live in a culture where people are easily thrown off by texts that are too wordy.

Outside the menu, strive to hire servers who can communicate articulately, and train your staff to avoid certain expressions.

Once in Toronto, as I waited in line for some delicious waffles covered in chocolate sauce, I witnessed the following dialogue:

—Ma'am, can I have a waffle please?

—I don't know, can you?

—Sorry?

—Oh, son, I apologize. I used to be an English teacher and just can't help myself.

—Sorry, ma'am. I'm American; we don't learn to speak English properly...

—Here's your waffle. Enjoy.


Since then, "Can I help you?" has been an expression that catches my attention.

Don't ask me "What can I do for you?" I don't know you; I'm not sure of what you are capable of doing for me. "What may I do for you?" will be semantically correct, but again, this vague question should be avoided.

"Is everything all right here?" is another nebulous attempt at showing attention. These types of questions often come at inopportune times, posed at the exact moment when I've taken a bite, making me rush to swallow without thoroughly chewing and causing a very uncomfortable chunky ball to travel through my esophagus, as if, in my distraction, I've swallowed a suppository instead of a pill. Food critic Gael Greene recommends that you simply say, "Please let me know if you require anything else," which doesn't demand a response on the client's part. Better yet, pay attention to the tables, and you will know if anything is missing. Check if the glasses are low on beverage, if the menus are folded on the table, if the plates are empty, if there is a missing set of silverware, or if a client has wandering eyes, suggesting that she is trying to find something. This will prompt you to make a much more specific offer to your client.

Pay attention to your words and the sense they make. I wouldn't really like the check, but I need you to bring it, please. The pepper is probably not fresh, but the grinding may be. Does "Good-bye, now" mean that you are rushing me out?

Why praise my choices? "Excellent choice, sir." Are the other choices in the menu not so good? Are you comparing my choice to your personal taste, or have some of the choices on the menu made people sick? If there are six of us at the table, will you rank us by our choices? Damn! I got a "good choice," but Pam got an "excellent choice." I should have thought it through better. That risotto she chose sounded very good indeed. Should I change my mind now?

I recently attended a lecture by Ferdinand Metz, former president of the Culinary Institute of America, and he mentioned finding it inappropriate to address clients, particularly more mature ones, by asking, "How are you guys doing?" There are moments when a bit of formality is adequate.

Another speaker, Larry Stewart, a well-regarded restaurant services consultant, mentioned that you should never, ever, use negative words. If your client asks for something, don't say, "No problem." Why would you want to bring the word "problem" to the conversation? Say, "Absolutely, I will be right back with your bread."

I actually do like the expression "y'all." I find that there is a linguistic need for a form of *you* clearly indicating to be in the plural. But, just like "you guys," unless you live in a region of the country where this is broadly accepted, this colloquialism implies informality and is restricted for use with a smaller demographic, so it's safer to avoid it.

You, naturally, in addition to choosing words and expressions carefully, want to enunciate words as clearly as possible and avoid slang and contractions. You are not on the streets with your buddies or at an MTV event. Clients expect you to display some propriety. This shows your level of respect for the client and also sets the tone for which the client will respond to you. Do an experiment and note how people react when you ask, "Ma'am, are you ready to order?" instead of "Ya ready?" My bet is that you'll raise a notch of courtesy and respect in the manner you are addressed back. You don't have to sound like an android; you can still be friendly and personal, while a bit more proper in language. It just may take some time getting used to.

Most importantly, never, under any circumstances, extend the last syllable of the last word in your sentences: "I'll pick up your drinks, and I'll be right back, okayyyyyyyeeeee?" This is annoying beyond any words I could possibly choose to describe it. I feel that I'm being treated like someone with a mental disturbance, or as if I look like someone who needs to be calmed down, or *niced* down. Stop this habit immediately. Seek aid from a speech therapist, if needed. This will change your life for the better in every possible aspect.

Finally, be genuine, and use the language as if you mean every word. If you ask, "How are you today?" say it as if you truly care about how I am. The strongest word in that question is *you*, not *are* or *today*, and that's how it should be said. Otherwise, instead of being mechanical, just skip the question altogether, greet us with "Good evening," and move on to taking the drinks order. There is a difference between being pleasantly nice and being noticeably fake nice, like many cosmetics demonstrators at department stores, telling my wife how wonderful she looks with the dark purple shade around her eyes. It looks horrendous; she looks like a brain-eating zombie in a bad sequel movie. Tell her that that color doesn't match her skin tone very well. It will win her trust, and I may give her another few minutes before dragging her out of the store.

# Psychic

As an auditor for a large public accounting firm, my most important client was a steel mill on the outskirts of Rio de Janeiro, in a small town where most of the population's livelihood, one way or another, revolves around its operation, similarly to many steel cities here in Pennsylvania a few decades ago. It was a straightforward, no-nonsense, blue-collar town. The food at the company's cafeteria frightened us, and our expenses were reimbursed, so we chose to eat at the hotel or at one of the two nearby restaurants.

Food at our three-star hotel—which possibly only deserved two—was OK. The waiters never wrote down the orders, nor ever brought what we had actually asked for, but it took them so astonishingly long to bring the food that we never returned a plate, fearing we would need another shave by the time we were done eating. We eventually learned to call in to order the food before we left the office and walked to the hotel's restaurant.

The other two restaurants weren't particularly stunning, but we had to vary our environment from time to time. They were what you would expect from a steel workers' town: no froufrou décor, pragmatic table settings, old-time servers, simple food, very large portions, and fair prices. Overall, what I would call honest meals.

One day at one of these restaurants, after we got our sodas and ordered our meals, knowing I'd be waiting for a bit, I glanced at the other tables, many still empty, checking if any table had an ashtray, indicating that smoking was welcome. At that time, you could have your puffs inside a restaurant, which I must now admit is inconsiderate to those who wisely chose not to smoke, as I have now chosen for many years.

Within a minute and without a word, the waiter laid an ashtray on my table. In shocked surprise, I rewound my brain and carefully examined the sequence of movements I had just made, and realized I never mentioned the words *smoke* or *cigarette*, I never pulled the pack or the lighter out of my jacket's pocket, and nothing on our table gave any indication that one of us was a smoker. I just glanced at the neighboring tables, and without too much alarm. Somehow, the server understood.

Now, that was a pretty cool Jedi Waiter move, to borrow a term used by the author of *Waiter Rant*. I said to my colleagues, "Wow, did you see that? Did you? Wasn't it cool?!" But they weren't remotely as amused as I was, possibly from annoyance that I was about to smoke around them.

I never asked the server how he did it. Maybe it was merely coincidence, but it couldn't have been, not really. I've now watched several other experienced servers in action; you can tell them from the rookies by their confidence and tranquility in the most chaotic service times. Good servers develop the capacity to observe, think, and react with cool heads and good judgment, as if they were Neo in *The Matrix*, with the scene running in slow motion. Achieving that level of mastery takes a learning curve and a good amount of emotional intelligence, combining knowledge and awareness.

In the business world I come from, a seasoned professional knows at what moment the boss will call, what she will ask, and what answer she will want to hear. You learn how people react to certain events and the timing of them. You also learn that the best way to save yourself from a surprising and embarrassing situation is to anticipate them. When you anticipate scenarios, you can react and resolve things quickly.

—Fernando, I just saw that our costs are up by 10 percent! What happened?

—We had technical issues with the implementation of module D, and our team is going to be at the client for another two months. However, we are trying to sell a change order to implement simultaneously, and its margin will make up for the additional costs. We will know the answer by next Wednesday, when our team has the weekly project meeting with the client's director.

Done. You sound like you know what you are talking about, and all questions are answered.

I bet that server had observed and dealt with so many clients that he knew exactly what I wanted simply by the way I glanced around. He probably also knew what I was going to order for my meal and dessert.

I mentioned before that good service goes unnoticed. Few things will make your service so great that we clients will actually perceive it; the ability to anticipate what your clients want or need is one of those few things. Bear in mind that guessing is a tricky business. Leave it to experienced professionals in a controlled setting, and don't try it at home. Don't make a fool of yourself saying, "Ma'am, you look like you want to order our Weight Watchers' certified low-calorie salad today." You can get physical injuries from making a bad call.

When I said that "Is everything okay here?" is a bad attempt at displaying attention to your clients, I meant that you should develop your awareness of what's going on around you. If Sue is flipping the menu back and forth in repeated and endless indecisive moves, she may want a prompt from you, like "Ma'am, if you'd like a recommendation from our menu, our most popular dish is the wasabi and honey-glazed grilled tofu. We also make our own fresh pasta, and the Shitake and Camembert ravioli is very successful with our clients." Be reasonable; don't just try to push your most expensive dish. Before you recommend, ponder the looks of my quite fit friend. Does she seem likely to order the one-pound burger with bacon and Cheez Whiz? If you pay attention to us, you will be able to narrow down the possibilities and impress us by bringing more bread or water, offering drinks at the right time, bringing extra plates and silverware, noticing the empty salt shaker or lack of napkins, before we even need to ask for any of that, or prompting some sinful desserts when we are hesitating to order them. When you get your attention in tune and the timing right, the Force will be with you.

# Please Don't Give Me that Face

All-you-can-eat buffets sound like a daring statement to me. "I dare you to fill up your plate with all the items we have, then repeat the ones you liked, and finally return for the ones you really liked." Boy, you don't know who you are messing with! I'm six-foot-three, 240 pounds, and I'm up to the challenge.

In forty-five minutes of lunch, I've done some serious damage to the buffet. It's an irrational behavior that the most barbaric of us engage in at these establishments. I feel regrettably sorry, and I feel guilty. I spent the first four days of the week on salads. I mean real salads, not the pepperoni, ham, bacon, and bleu cheese type of "salad." I exercised twice and lost almost a full pound. All vainly wasted with the bestial instinct of a wild boar and pure lack of self-control.

That very same Friday, I'm meeting with friends at a very pleasant Mediterranean café, one of my favorite restaurants in the area. I really can't eat much. Or maybe I could, but I won't. Not this time. I grew up as a Roman Catholic, and we are very well trained in guilt. Gluttony is one of the seven capital sins, and if I indulge again, on the very same day, I'm sure I won't be welcomed anywhere nice in my afterlife.

The other three people at the table place fair orders of soups, shared appetizers, and entrées, but I'll have to go for a soup and a small salad at most or just an appetizer. I feel guilty again, but for a different reason. It's a busy night, and I know the server is hoping for a big check. I try to apologetically explain my earlier insanity at the Indian buffet, but at that point I have already convinced myself that the waitress hates me. I imagine the server wondering why she was so unfortunate to not get the other four people that sat at table fourteen, and she is convinced that the hostess is boycotting her, probably due to some misunderstanding about the hostess' boyfriend. They are better dressed at table fourteen, look wealthier, and will certainly all order full meals and desserts. She got the cheap one. I just ruined the night for this nice woman attending us. It's all in my head. The server has not moved a single facial muscle, but I can't help it. I'm paranoid, and I hear voices.

As a personal favor, please give me some reassurance that it's okay. You've done it, too, I'm sure. At least once in your life you were too full or ended up in a place you couldn't afford. Please don't make me feel worse than I already feel. Please don't give me that face.

I'll tip you a bit more, I promise, and next time I will have a full meal. But if you give me a face, I'll be too embarrassed to return, which will be particularly regrettable because I quite like this restaurant.

Several years ago, I made a trip to Williamsburg, Virginia. It's a delightful journey, a travel in time back to early America, where through the well-preserved and reconstructed historical setting, you can relive the lifestyle and culture of the time when we fought to become an independent nation. I went for dinner at a restaurant out of the historical compound. The place didn't look like much from the outside, but had some very self-confident prices on the menu, and my budget then didn't include a provision for $30 to $50 plates. After we ordered appetizers, two of us intended to share an entrée, and we were told that the house rules require that every guest orders a main dish, no exceptions. Power to you if you can get away with it. Maybe in Williamsburg, as a tourist place, the restaurants don't count on returning clients. But, were it close to where I live, they would never see me back. Even when this book has earned me a fortune than makes Warren Buffet envious, I just can't tolerate this arrogant attitude.

I have a few friends too, and you know people talk. In these tough economic times, I wouldn't scare any client away; a small check is certainly better than an empty table.

You know how it goes. It's significantly easier to retain a client than to conquer new ones. Or, in the words of Thomas Jefferson, who went to school in Williamsburg, "An injured friend is the bitterest of foes."

# The Ship Was Attacked by Pirates

An experienced chef once told me that he was going out for dinner with his girlfriend the next evening. As you can imagine, chefs are very critical when they go out to eat. Cooks often receive simple homemade food well, somewhat as a relief from some over-elaborated and often unhealthy recipes we cook for the public. But when we go to restaurants, we judge. We look for creative ideas and check if plates are better executed than the ones we make.

The following day, I asked him how it went. "Disappointing," he said. He went to a new and trendy fusion restaurant, which had an ambitious menu. He found ostrich as one of the specialties, which seemed exciting to him, and not having eaten that meat in a while, my chef friend ordered it.

"Sorry," the waiter said, "we don't have it today. As a matter of fact, we hardly ever have it. I don't even know why they keep it on the menu!"

From that point on, he knew the service wouldn't go well. He began noticing service flaws, like lack of knowledge of the menu, confusion in taking orders, and delivering the plates to the incorrect position at the table.

It happens to all of us at some point, having a job that sucks. I hated my first job with all my heart. It was in a big public accounting firm. Beyond the boring work and low pay, the partners managing the subsidiary were mean and stingy to the point that there weren't enough chairs for us at the office during the low season, when most of us were actually in the office instead of at clients' facilities, so we had to take turns sitting. I endured three and a half painful years there, to build up my CV and for the professional experience. One thing I learned from more seasoned colleagues is that it's a bad idea to talk openly about the place you work for, especially with clients. If nothing else, it reflects poorly on you. You will look like a whining, disgruntled employee, who can't find anything better than the very crappy job you are complaining about. It makes you look like a loser. Many of us auditors eventually got recruited by our clients for better jobs and higher pay. For us to be attractive, our company had to look good, so the world believed that by hiring us, they were hiring the absolute best. That belief was true, by the way. Despite the miserable working conditions, we were known for being the very best audit firm, due to the one thing the partners didn't pinch pennies on: training.

So the owner insists on keeping ostrich on the menu because it looks exotic, but he can't have regular deliveries of it. If someone orders the dish, you should tell us the *truth*: "I'm so terribly sorry! This is one of our most popular items. We buy the meat directly from an ostrich farmer in New Zealand. He ships it in small carbon-neutral sailboats, and last week the boat was attacked by Somali pirates. We served our last ostrich fillets during lunch today. May I suggest the duck confit? We just received a fresh shipment of duck from our Canadian supplier, who raises them on an organic farm outside Montreal. We also received spectacular fresh fois gras from this same farm."

# If You Just Smile

One thing I like about French movies is they don't bother to explain things to those of us who are a bit slow or had to go out for a popcorn refill. Hollywood movies want to make sure you understood what you saw. No matter how simplistic the plot, the studios feel compelled to spend the last five minutes explaining what happened in the previous ninety and wrap it up with a message. There will be a narrator's closing remarks, a speech at a trial, a wedding showing how all characters will go on, a criminal genius or degenerated policeman explaining the minimal details of his evil plan to a captured hero. I find it humiliatingly condescending. I'd rather just pretend that I understood, as I usually do after I watch a David Lynch movie.

I watched the original French version of *La Femme Nikita* in 1990. The movie is directed by Luc Besson, and has impeccable performances by Anne Parillaud and Tchéky Karyo. If you have only watched the series on TV or the American version with Bridget Fonda, I suggest you give the French version a shot. There are no explanations whatsoever. No one knows what caused her to become that angered punk in the opening scene or what kind of organization turned her into a professional assassin. You may conclude it's some kind of government agency, but no one will spoon-feed you your conclusions. At the end, you don't know what's going to become of her, nor of any other characters that still happen to be alive by then.

I particularly like one scene, where Nikita has an "appointment" with an older lady, who acts as some sort of social etiquette consultant. The session was part of the agency's effort to reshape Nikita into a human being. The lady looks like she's had a rough life herself, and her expression indicates that she understands what Nikita is going through, but she doesn't let Nikita believe that there will be any camaraderie or tolerance of violations of her strict rules. Nikita has her usual angry face, but she's surrounded with sophisticated objects and classical music, and shows discomfort with this environment. The lady asks Nikita:

—What's the definition of *grace*?

—I'm not smart.

—Smile, then. That'll be a good start. Smile when you don't know something. It won't make you any smarter, but it will be more pleasant for the others.

Smiling works. I've done it all my life, even in business meetings with the grumpiest people. You enter your boss' office and offer an honest, kind smile, ask if he's feeling better from the flu. That breaks the ice. Then your face can be serious again. With a sorry look you can say, "I'm afraid I do not have good news. I just looked at the sales report and the numbers are very disappointing. That expected large contract was postponed for a few months."

Very few people will mistreat you when you are pleasant and offer a generous smile. When I go to restaurants, I try to be nice and smile at the servers; they often smile back. Sometimes you'll be the one who has to start.

# Try This Soup

A man goes into the restaurant, and he sits down. He's having a bowl of soup. He says to the waiter: "Waiter, come taste this soup."

The waiter asks, "Is something wrong with the soup?"

—Just taste the soup.

—Is there something wrong with the soup? Is the soup too hot?

—Just, will you taste the soup?

—What's wrong? Is the soup too cold?

—Will you taste the soup?!

—All right, I'll taste the soup! Where's the spoon?

—Aha! Ahaaa!

This joke is at the end of Eddie Murphy's comedy film *Coming to America*, directed by John Landis. If 1988 sounds pretty old for your generation, think of it as a classic. Go ahead and rent it. Eddie Murphy was at the top of his career and plays four characters in the movie. I would rate it as a chick flick that guys would be OK with. The movie was nominated for Academy Awards in costume design and makeup.

If there were a scale of gaffe severity, I believe this missing spoon would be high on the list. Note that I wouldn't rank poor hygiene and bad sanitary practices as gaffes; those would be negligence. When the food arrives before the silverware, it's a strong sign of disorganization and inattention, no matter whose responsibility it was to bring the silverware, whether the host's, busboy's, or server's. Before food comes, the server has already been to the table at least twice, probably more, and every staff member has had multiple opportunities to note that there is something missing. Of course, we all get distracted and make mistakes, and we shouldn't make a big fuss of unintentional mishaps, but the situation might indicate a chronic, systematic inattentiveness and dysfunctional teamwork.

I understand the staff is busy and multitasking, but a server must be aware of a few basic items. Do the clients have menus? Did you take their orders? Do they have drinks? Do they have silverware? Are they done eating? The server ought to be checking all the time. Every time she passes by, she should glance by to see if anything looks odd. Managers, hosts, and busboys, too. Let your peers know if you notice something out of order in their tables. Restaurants are not a place for "This is not my job" silliness. It's a team effort, and you watch each other's backs.

It will be easier to see what's going on if you keep the tables neat and clear. I would not keep on the table anything not absolutely indispensable: plate, silverware, salt and pepper, and menu. Possibly a tent display for the desserts. Candles, lamps, and flower vases take precious room that could be needed to accommodate the plates. Also, they usually make ineffective decorations, especially if the candleholders are cheap (and the fire code won't allow you to light them) and the flowers are plastic. If your tables are very large and you have gorgeous glass sculptures from Murano for decoration, you may be fine.

Salt and pepper are essential to keep on the table. Craig, a colleague at cooking school, works for a chef who removed all the salt shakers from the tables, under the premise that food should come perfectly seasoned from the kitchen. I think it's bullshit. I like more salt than average, so let me deal with my wife's disapproval on that. You are wasting my time as I try to find salt around the restaurant while my food gets cold. If you're in a sophisticated restaurant, bottled steak sauce and ketchup will be inappropriate, but a small bottle of fine hot sauce would be okay with me and shouldn't offend most chefs.

Other items must come with specific needs: syrup jars for pancakes, garlic-infused olive oil for bread, sweetener for coffee, and so on. Build a mental process to automatically check things as you pass through the tables. Now if someone older than forty asks you to try their food, you know what he means.

# Buddhism

Siddhartha Gautama presumably lived between 485 BC and 400 BC, in the border region of modern-day India and Nepal. Born in a family of regional royalty, the Buddha experimented with both luxurious comfort at his family's palace and uttermost deprivation in his ascetic quest for spiritual realization. He later recognized that a moderate path was the one that would lead him to enlightenment. Once enlightened, he taught his disciples the "four noble truths:" there is suffering in the world, suffering is caused by attachment to things, suffering can be ended, and the way to end it is a path of righteousness and mindfulness.

I am moved by the Buddhist philosophy, which I don't interpret as a religion, but as a way of approaching life, independent of what someone believes about a deity. It encouraged me to become vegetarian, to be more mindful of my misbehaviors, and to spend more time living in the present.

The philosophy teaches us that all things in life are transitory and forever changing. Our continual dissatisfaction comes from the persistence in clinging to things and ideas. Once we learn to live in the present and accept the fleeting nature of the world, we are liberated.

One of the material things I have learned to not cling to is silverware. I believe we must let go of our forks and knives between courses and allow them to follow their natural cycle, returning, refreshed, for the next stage of our dining experience.

Unfortunately, too many restaurants want me to hold on to the same set of silverware throughout the entire meal, which I find appalling for many reasons.

- You brought me a clean and sanitized set of silverware wrapped or on top of a clean napkin. Once the napkin is on my lap and you take the plate from my appetizer away, I won't have a clean place to rest my silverware, so I may have to rest it on the table, which may not be entirely sanitary.

- After I finish my appetizer, my silverware will be dirty. As I finish my eggplant Parmesan, I will either have to aggressively lick the marinara sauce off the fork, clean it on the napkin—dirtying the napkin—or stain your tablecloth.

- The residue of marinara sauce may add undesired flavor to my next course. The beautiful creamy white sauce will be stained with red tomato sauce.

- It is unpleasant to view dirty silverware or anything else dirty sitting on the table.

I believe it's a cheap practice for a restaurant of any level of sophistication not to replace silverware. You should take it away after each course, no questions asked.

I also require a full set of utensils: fork, knife, and spoon. Each piece of flatware has its own history of evolution in shape and material, dating back to prehistoric times, when forks and knives were made out of bones and wood, and spoons out of shells, clay, or anything else remotely concave. Spoons are for liquids and semi-liquids, like soups and soft mousse, and for serving and stirring. Many people use them to assist in rolling spaghetti around the fork, but I don't find it necessary, nor do I have the required skills for that. Forks are for most eating, and knives are for cutting and helping to load the fork. I frequently receive a course with only a fork, like a salad. I will need a knife to cut a tomato wedge too large for politely fitting in my mouth, and I was taught that nibbling foods from the fork is inappropriate table etiquette. The knife also helps foods onto the fork, so that I don't have to use my fingers to push the loose peas. The practice of bringing full sets of silverware is good for you, too. If I get my fingers dirty pushing food onto the fork, among the possibilities for cleaning them are the linen, the seat, the wall, the menu cover, etc.

For desserts, good etiquette is to serve it with both a fork and a spoon. The fork is intended for the primary eating, while the spoon aids bits onto the fork. The spoon also comes in handy for non-solids, like the melting ice cream on the side of the pie. The spoon is not the best tool for the pie itself, because it doesn't cut through the crust very well, nor is it ergonomically designed to allow the piece of pie to slide easily into your mouth. For obvious reasons, the fork is inadequate for eating ice cream. As I learned in my ventures in home improvement projects and in culinary school, there's a best tool for every job.

Having different sizes and shapes of silverware for different dishes adds a touch of elegance. We have all become accustomed to the practicality of using the same shape of fork for everything—including fish and seafood, meats, and desserts—so it's unlikely that many people will be disappointed for not receiving a proper fish fork. I realize it's part of the ambience and ritual, but I can't help finding it a bit amusing to get a special enormous serrated knife for meats. Does it indicate that your regular knife is worthless or that the meat will be tough?

Now, while we're on the topic of Buddhist awareness and tabletop etiquette, here's another issue I must mention: you already do your best that all plates should arrive at the table at the same time. You don't want to make people uncomfortable for starting to eat before everybody else is served, nor to force people to wait, staring at their plates, while someone still waits for hers. Don't overlook that the same rule applies to removing the plates. You should wait until everyone finishes to remove the plates, so that someone still eating, like my friend Chang who eats abnormally slowly, doesn't feel rushed or realizes that he has been left to eat alone.

For those who do receive their plates before the other parties at the table, the guideline is that it's acceptable to start eating when at least two people are served, so that your food doesn't get cold and you don't make the unserved people uncomfortable because others are waiting on them. Waiting with patience is, of course, a good Zen trait, but not all of us are enlightened.

# The Check

When I mentioned to Teresa, a good friend whose family owns restaurants in Mexico, that I was writing this book, she quickly reacted, "You must say something about them bringing the check before I ask for it!"

I ran a quick survey and learned that this goes unnoticed by my American friends, but most of my foreign friends find it offensive, in varying degrees from "Yeah, it's a bit weird" to "I feel like they are kicking me out."

I never saw this practice in other countries, but I have now gotten used to it. Also, meals are expected to take much longer abroad. Here, we are pressed to finish rather rapidly, to get back to our desks at work or to relieve the babysitter at night. In Brazil, a lunch break rarely takes less than one hour, and in Spain or Mexico, at least two hours, which made my American boss quite anxious during our international business trips. Dinner is a social event in almost every culture, involving drinks, appetizers, a main course or courses, and dessert, and it's generally expected to be a longer occasion.

In the United States, we have been conditioned to obsess about work and to feel guilty when we leave our offices for long. We forgot that having a break during the day is healthy for the mind, and that we can even be more productive in the afternoon if we chill during lunch. Instead, we learned to eat as fast as possible, and we encouraged restaurants to operate like fast food. Thus, it is our fault that many restaurants rush to give us the check. Many people seem to appreciate it as good customer service. I told Teresa that this practice doesn't bother me too much these days. It certainly doesn't look very classy, though, and most certainly it shuts down our willingness to order coffee and dessert.

Many servers carry a current check printout of each of their tables in their aprons, in case the client asks for it. This way certainly handles the need for expediency better without pressing the patron.

Now, I do really appreciate here in America that the servers hardly ever take the tip cash while you are still at the table. This is a proper gesture of discretion. In most other countries, the waiter will rush to take the pay while you still sit at the table, or the clients will make sure, as they stand up and prepare to leave, that the waiter noticed them leaving and that they left money on the table. In Brazil, unattended cash vanishes instantly.

I absolutely discourage the practice of bringing a partial check when the waiter's shift ends or he needs to leave early. We clients, more often than not, understand and will comply with the request, but it looks very unprofessional. You should be friends with at least one other server and be able to ask her the favor of closing your table, trusting that she will not rip you off and keep your money. See, the structure of the shifts and the fact that you must leave are not a client's problem. As in any other business situation, you deal with your problems internally and do the uttermost not to bring them to light to your clients.

I have friends who like to split the bill evenly and others who like to pay specifically for what they ordered. When someone like me orders several drinks and dessert and other people eat like birds, dividing the sum evenly by the number of people would be unfair. On these occasions, it helps to have a detailed check, legible and in plain English, not in Chinese Han characters or in any form of waiter shorthand. Checks should always be clearly readable, allowing the more skeptical of us to check the math and detailed contents.

Last, I would like to apologize to servers for the many times I have, and probably still will, put you to the trouble of splitting the check over several credit cards, with different amounts on each. I acknowledge it's a pain in the ass, but we live in a world of plastic money, and few people carry much cash these days.

# Value

Karl Marx's theory of exploitation of the workforce contains a core concept: *value* and *price* are different things. *Value* is what something costs, in labor and materials, to be produced; *price* is what the product is sold for in the market. The difference between the two equals the profit, in which the capitalist would be exploiting the worker. Marx then gets confused in the mathematical model, expressing the value of labor and materials by their market prices, which creates a spiraling contradiction in the theory. Of course, we all know how miserably communism failed as governing and economic systems, discouraging innovation and competition and proliferating a corrupt cast of bureaucrats. What is still of relevance, although with a slightly different interpretation, is that Value and Price are indeed different things.

As I'm writing this book, the electronic tablets market is booming, split between the iPad and the competing Androids. I haven't yet found a need for a tablet in my personal routine, because I type better on my notebook and my smart phone is more practical to carry. My friend Lance tells me that it's the ultimate toilet companion, but I guess I'm still a paper-based, old-fashioned bathroom reader. I've played around with the tablets, found them pretty neat, but I wouldn't know what to do with them, so I turned away from a couple of good deals for buying them. When something has little value to you, its price means little.

I focus on functionality and price, while my wife values style and branding. She uses the price as an indicator of quality, a relationship she sometimes assumes correctly, and she invariably suggests we buy the most expensive option for anything. "Dear, I know for fact that the detergent's supermarket brand and the name brand are manufactured by the same company in the same line. It's exactly the same product." She glances at me, incredulous, and picks up the name brand from the shelf. Now, even if price and quality always had a direct relationship, the relationship between price and value may be less direct. If you are buying a very good 9.5° driver for golf, an optional shaft covered in gold will not make you shoot longer or straighter, and the rise in price will not match the rise in value, unless you value showing off your golden club.

In the same way, clients will have varying perceptions of value and of the prices they are willing to pay for stuff. The perceived value of your product will determine your business' viability and ability to support your pricing, but establishing your prices is a multi-dimensional process relating to the scale of values of your clients, the wealth and habits of the demographic, and the prices of your competition. You may charge $30 per plate under certain conditions, but you won't be able to charge that much for the same plate at a different location with a different client demographic. In a different scenario, charging too little for your product may damage the perceived value by your clients, implying that your food is inferior.

Once you have defined your target clients, fine-tuned your product offering, and priced them according to your marketplace, you may be considering a promotion to bring people in to try your food. Be careful. Coupons, special offers, and other pricing promotions are a tricky business from a value perception standpoint. They have the potential to become the routinely perceived price, rather than the exceptional deal, and you will be sending a confusing message.

Let's say, for the purpose of illustration, that I am comfortable with paying $14.95 for a high quality all-you-can-eat lunch buffet. You want to be able to charge $19.95, but you launch a grand opening promotion at half price, $9.95, to attract the public. It may effectively fill your restaurant, but you aren't necessarily making money or attracting the right demographic. As soon as your full price takes effect, many of us will be gone. You may have to consider another promotion, making the prices look schizophrenic and your client base unstable. Be careful with the expectations you set and how that influences our perception of value. Once I've paid $9.95, I'll be reluctant to pay more at a later time. Once you get stuck at charging $9.95, your business plan changes completely, due to the quality of food and service you can afford and the volume you need to sell.

This doesn't mean that you shouldn't use promotions; just make sure to define your objectives and plan your campaigns accordingly. Options proven to be effective are specific exceptional promotions, like free-tenth-meal fidelity cards, early-bird specials, and simplified lunch menus. They target specific demographics that would raise business for you. I personally believe that if you charge less for a meal during a low occupancy shift, your menu should be different, so I don't get confused between the value of your food and the value of your space, and how you charge for them.

The same concern with messing with my expectations goes for portion sizes. American portions are often gargantuan and even I am incapable of finishing a four-course meal: appetizer, soup, entrée, and dessert. My spouse and I like to try each other's plates, and we share dishes. For example, we might order two large appetizers, one soup, one entrée, and one dessert, or whatever combination of interesting plates we find on the menu. You may find it inconvenient that we share plates and may decide to reduce the size of the appetizers to encourage your clients to order individual starters and main courses. I assure you that we will notice the smaller size and, if your prices haven't been reduced for the smaller portions, I will be pissed off.

Luckily for you, restaurants have one great option for discreetly adjusting prices, portion sizes, or both: change the menu. You can create a whole set of new dishes to redefine your prices. I recommend that you make sure to keep the dishes that made you successful and to introduce reasonable changes from your clients. If you used to have a fried calamari starter, enough for two people, at $10.95, you will be pushing it by charging $8.95 for a reduced portion of your new saffron calamari rings, but you may be able to charge $6.95 for this "half portion." If this encourages people to order their individual starters, you just got an extra $3 per deuce and gave me a chance of trying different appetizers with my wife. Another option is to replace the appetizer with the same-sized Hawaiian Coconut Calamari for two and charge $12.95. It may fly.

One of the Indian restaurants nearby drastically reduced the portions of rice that accompany the dishes. Indian food has a lot of sauce, and I don't know how to eat it without abundant rice and naan bread. After they reduced the portion, we always had to ask for more rice halfway through our meal. Indian restaurants are notoriously slow, so invariably the sauce would be cold by the time we received the extra rice. We eventually decided to change our choice of Indian restaurants for their competitor, a few hundred feet down the road.

Be careful not to mess too much with my cheese, for it will freak me out. I created a perception of value for your restaurant in my mind and also associated it with a certain price range and portion size. I don't like having stuff taken away from me, in the same manner that I cannot convince my wife to downgrade our cable plan. I guess she's too much of a bourgeoisie. In Marx's world, we'd have only one channel, probably not very interesting in content, but completely free.

# Unleash the Home Run

I am not a huge fan of baseball. I like the game, but I lack the attention span for an event that lasts an average of two hours and fifty minutes, played by the same team for as many as fifteen consecutive days. A fanatical baseball fan, determined to demonstrate both steadfast commitment and miraculous endurance, would devote 460 hours, the equivalent to twenty full days, to watch all games of her favorite team during the regular season of 162 games, not including the pre- and post-game commentaries. Such devotion is not for me, but I enjoy actually going to the park a few times per season and watching the Phillies through the playoffs, when they make it there.

When I was living in Pittsburgh, a friend told me that the Pirates offered one-dollar tickets for select games. One dollar is almost free and, well, free is hard to beat. Calling a Pirates vs. Blue Jays match a "select game" is indeed a euphemism, but the PNC is a beautiful park, and it's nice to be out at a ball game in the spring. Undoubtedly, being at the game changes the experience. You get to watch the warm-up batting practice, join the choir of fans, and enjoy the refreshingly gratifying opportunity of paying nine dollars for a plastic cup of Bud Light.

The Pirates weren't at their most glorious, holding the longest streak in the Major Leagues for not making it to the playoffs: eighteen years. I suppose that explains why the dollar-tickets were largely unsuccessful in filling the stadium that evening. The stadium was about one quarter full, most of the people sitting in the higher tiers. It was a sad sight, and it was also sad to hear comments that minor league games had been twice as full.

During the seventh inning stretch, we went out for our last beer and for a walk around the park, which none of us had visited before. By the bottom of the 8th, we decided to help ourselves to better seats at a lower tier, in a section that would seat 500 people and at that moment had about 10 occupying it. Pittsburgh was losing badly, and the scarce crowd had started to leave the park. A few moments later, a diligent usher escorted us out of the seats, relieving the area of our undignified presence.

The question, of course, is why? I know, I know, so that people who actually paid to be in that section didn't feel cheated, but, really, why? Why would you chose to enforce the seating rules and piss off four guys who actually chose to go to the game, on a evening when the whole of Pittsburg decided they had better things to do? Why would you deny us a taste of watching, from better seats, the home team be humiliated through the last inning? For whom are they saving those seats? For the folks that clearly aren't coming out?

That same year, I agreed to go to George Michael concert in Philly, conditional on purchasing the cheapest tickets available, from which, my wife protested, we would barely be able to discern the man's dance moves (which turned out to bit quite agile for his age). As we got to the stadium, we were greeted with the news that the event didn't sell out, and we had all been upgraded. We were handed new tickets, for the club boxes. When George Michael came to the stage, he said, "Thank you for being a George Michael fan. I know I've made it hard for you to be my fan." It resulted in a great show. I had a really good time and definitely enjoyed the perk of the upgraded seating. Quite a different experience from the one at the PNC stadium.

Instead of watching baseball, I've spent many evenings watching Gordon Ramsay's *Kitchen Nightmares*, the show where the Scottish chef visits struggling restaurants and candidly tells the owners why they're failing. American and British television have their own versions of the show. If you ignore the theatrics, the program is very informative, and you can learn many lessons from it.

One of the most remarkable recurring issues is the habit of excessive pre-cooking in virtually deserted restaurants. Why would you bother to pre-cook food in a slow business? Just so that the eventual clients will have the pleasure to eat food that sat for hours on the steam table or was cooled to be reheated in the microwave? For whom are you saving the fresh cooking and the good stuff? The Pirates' fans?

Unleash your arm and hit a food home run for the folks coming to your restaurant. Hit it, man, hit it long!

# Decadence

When I was in my teens, a small family-owned bakery made the best dessert I ever had—a three-layer chocolate mousse, dark, sweet, and white, over a super-thin crispy chocolate crust. What made it so delicious was each individual mousse, a heavenly manifestation of perfection that balanced with scientific precision the ratio of chocolate, cream, eggs, and sugar, and resisted the temptation of adding stuff that didn't belong there: no raspberry, orange zest, mint, coffee, or anything else people like to add to chocolate to give it a kick. When it comes to chocolate, I'm a purist. I want to taste the chocolate and just the chocolate. In fact, I'm gradually becoming a vegan, so even milk and eggs are also becoming unwanted additions. That dessert was a huge success, and it raised the standards for the birthday cakes for my friends' celebrations.

I hadn't been to that shop for a long while, where the artisanal desserts were wonders of the world. It was located in a large food market, similar to the Reading Terminal Market in Philadelphia.

A few months ago I was in the neighborhood, and promised my wife that if the store was still there, she was in for a treat. She would have the best dessert of her life!

Salivating like Pavlov's dog, I rushed through the maze of produce and food vendors and, to my great excitement, the store was still there. Great news! The not-so-great news was that it looked different. What used to be a bakery that only sold pies, tarts, and cakes had become a small deli. It sold everything from cheeses and cold meats to canned food and spices. Not a good sign. They wouldn't be slicing ham and Swiss cheese if the pie business was doing well.

Let me illustrate the impression I got from that changed business. Imagine that once you conceived a charming and cozy coffee shop where you could earn your livelihood while making the world a little better. Your place was a refuge for people to unwind from daily stress, enjoy the best coffee on earth and make new friends, or just browse the Internet or read a magazine. Your coffee grains were of premium quality, freshly roasted, and ground just before brewing. You made sure to buy fair-trade coffee so your heart could be at peace, and your clients appreciated the effort. Your pastries were your grandma's recipes, and you baked a fresh batch every morning right before you opened. A few months after you opened, you realize the business does not generate as much sales as expected because there are three other coffee shops within a mile radius, and a fast food chain is selling a large cup of premium flavored coffee for 99¢ to promote their breakfast hours. You love your shop, but times are tough. You can't afford another employee, so you're working insane hours, seven days a week.

Your best friend Suzy has an idea. She met a sexy Italian guy on a train in Tuscany who is a sales representative of a gorgeous and stylish brand of Italian shoes. She can give Giancarlo a call and see if she can be the exclusive distributor of the brand in the United States. She could share the space of the coffee shop with you and split the rent. The concept of selling exclusive shoes in a coffee house atmosphere somehow seems pretty cool to you: why hasn't anybody thought of that? What woman wouldn't like to buy shoes there?

You went along with the plan, and now shoe boxes are everywhere, compromising kitchen space, storage, and the sitting area. You had agreed to help each other so that each of you could have more free personal time, but Suzy can't bake a cookie to save her life, and you can't stand the indecisiveness of some of the shoe buyers. You continue to not sell much coffee, nor can Suzy sell enough shoes. Your relationship grows bitter. Suzy convinces you that buying frozen pastries from a major distributor would make your lives much easier and that buying another brand of ground coffee would add some 20 percent profit per cup. She also added other types of shoes to the product offerings, nowhere near the quality of the Italian shoes, but the new shoes are half the price. Your cousin, who lives in Oregon, is in town. She comes by the shop and plainly tells you that the concept doesn't feel right and that she wouldn't go there for a coffee if she lived in the neighborhood, because the store doesn't feel cozy anymore. The relaxing atmosphere is gone. You created a monster.

That is how I felt at the dessert shop. A few of the original pies sat in the refrigerated counter, squeezed between a jar of pickles and a container with smoked salmon spread. It didn't feel right, but at least my three-layer-mousse tart was there, still a reason for rejoicing. I got a couple of slices, sat down to dig my fork in, took a bite, and the whole world collapsed like a 2012 Mayan prophecy. It was terrible. In the context of chocolate mousse, let me be clear about what terrible is: cornstarch and gelatin. Cornstarch and gelatin are thickeners, more stable than the egg whites and cream emulsion, and they give desserts a much longer shelf life. They also make a crappy mousse. In fact, once you use cornstarch and gelatin, it's no longer a mousse; it's a pudding. I have tasted good puddings, but none would qualify as the best dessert ever. Also, gelatin is made out of bones and is not vegetarian, and I wasn't expecting it.

So there it was, one of my best memories ruined. Like when you go visit the house you lived in when you were seven and realize it's actually much smaller than you remember, or you come across a high school muse from your senior year, and she's no longer cute; her traits became rough and so did her manners, as if life took away the best in her.

That store still stood open, twenty years later, possibly for one reason; its spectacular tarts once meant something to people. I understand the need to change and adapt to new realities, but if you are going to change the fundamental essence of who you are, you might as well pen a whole new business with a different name. A fundamental change causes disappointment. Maybe I would have bought at your deli if you had opened a deli, but you continue to present yourself as a dessert shop, and the disappointment is enormous. I'm heartbroken.

Writing about the decadence of my favorite tart has sunk me into deep depression, I need to ease my mind. I guess I'm going out to have a cup of coffee and buy some Italian shoes. I know just the place.

# Ninety-Nine Cents

Data overwhelmingly supports that pricing items a penny short of the next dollar, a practice known in marketing as "odd pricing," affects consumers' conscious and unconscious buying habits. One well-publicized research study was conducted in 1996 by Robert Schindler, PhD, and Thomas Kibarian, then a student at the Wharton School of Business. Their research was conducted among ninety thousand customers of a catalog sales retailer during the winter clearance catalog edition. Thirty thousand randomly selected customers received catalogs with identical items, but with prices ending in 99¢, versus thirty thousand customers whose catalogs with the prices rounded to the next full dollar. The sales to the customers who got catalogs with prices ending in 99¢ were 8 percent higher. Surprisingly, the sales to the final thirty thousand customers, who received catalogs with prices ending in 88¢, resembled the sales from the catalogs with prices rounded to the next dollar, rather than the sales from the catalogs with prices ending in 99¢.

The research concluded that consumers interpret that odd prices ending in 99¢ reflect an effort to reduce prices to the lowest possible level. Additionally, now that we have become used to such odd prices, we find it unusual to see prices rounded up.

Other psychological factors that seem to contribute to consumers' illusory receptiveness for the 1¢ discounts are:

- **Initial point of focus.** We read from left to right, top to bottom. Marketers learned that the most important content in any material must be displayed at the top left quadrant of the page and reinforced at the bottom right. You should never start the page with blah-blah-blah and bury your appealing message in the center of the text. For the same reason, we also better perceive and retain the first characters of any word or number, so we automatically interpret that the nine in $9.99 as a better deal than the ten in $10.00, taking another nanosecond to realize that one penny is not worth driving an extra mile or compromising for less quality.

- **Guilty consumers.** We spend money on stupid stuff, like a $9.99 garlic peeler. I was young and too naïve to realize that you only have to press the garlic clove against the cutting board with the blade of your chef's knife, saving the effort of finding the peeler. After spending money on some useless gadget, I compensate by saving pennies, like in how I buy gasoline. My car drinks 91 octane gasoline, which is hard to find at most gas stations. When my wife isn't watching, I fill half the tank with 89 and the remainder with 93 octane. I'm convinced it works perfectly, while she believes the car will spectacularly explode into a million pieces. It saves me some 60¢ per fill.

- **Principle.** Some people claim to do things just for the principle. I, for one, tend to buy the lowest-priced brand of indistinguishable commodities, because I believe it sends the right message to the industry.

- **Worthwhile effect.** A penny here and a penny there add up. I worked for a company owned by a man whose personal wealth I estimated to be around three quarters of a billion dollars. He drives an old car and hasn't bought clothes for twenty-five years. Although I believe there's a disconnect between the millions of dollars his company makes and the savings from not buying a new pair of shoes, I have admiration for those who resist the temptations of unnecessary spending and feed their piggy bank regularly and generously.

- **Bragging rights.** Some of us love to find great deals and brag about them, displaying our smarts in negotiation and price finding. I particularly like buying returned electronic merchandise and brag that my fifty-inch TV cost me 20 percent less than the one in the unopened box. And it still works perfectly, after six years.

So what's my problem with the 99¢ pricing? Not the pricing itself, though I find it a bit silly to pretend that single cents can add up to something material. I am from a generation that hasn't known days when you could actually buy anything with a penny. When I was born, a first class stamp cost 6¢, and you couldn't buy a single piece of chewing gum for 1¢. A penny will not make a difference, regardless of what they say in the advertisements of long-distance phone services. All the pennies you saved in a lifetime of 99¢ prices will not afford you better retirement or pay for your kids' college.

My real problem is nothing ever results in a round figure after you apply the sales tax. The US is the only country I know where the sales tax is not embedded in the displayed price. Anywhere else, as you wait in line to order a meal number six, you can pull the money from your wallet with exact change or know how much your change will be. Here, unless you have the supernatural arithmetic skills of an autistic genius, you must wait for the register to process your sales tax to find out that your total is $8.04. This may explain why the fellow ahead of me in line waits until the very last moment to reach for his pocket and struggle to extract the wallet from a tight pair of pants, as if laboring to give birth to a fifteen-pounder. Wallet found, next comes the scanning for a $10 bill he could swear he had in the morning.

My esteemed reader, I have a personal request. Regardless of how you price your items, I beg you to join me in this campaign: never again give 99¢ for change. Ever. If you are a customer, boycott those who engage in this practice. My preferred boycott target has been the Blockbuster movie rental stores. I've used the services of the now-suicidal Netflix almost from the moment of its inception, but sometimes I'm not diligent in organizing the queue. We receive some strange batch of black-and-white German documentaries, which I selected in a moment of deep depression, and I decide I need something a bit more thrilling for a Friday night. On those occasions, I would revisit my friends at a surviving Blockbuster store, where the rental movies used to cost $4.02 after taxes. After the first time I had to stick 98¢ in my pocket, I decided to no longer pay in cash. It's a pain in the ass; the best you can do for 98¢ is three quarters, two dimes, and three pennies. Eight coins, man!

It is mostly a guy thing to hate coins. Fashion evolved in such manner that guys don't carry handbags, except for very self-assured metrosexuals with their Italian shoulder wallets. Come to think of it, handbags would be quite convenient, avoiding bent sunglasses and unintentional phone calls to my ex-girlfriend at odd hours, but I'm still too self-conscious to carry a handbag with me in current fashion. The dingling of coins in my pocket is annoying, and they all fall on my bedroom floor when I remove my pants, forcing me to bend and contour myself into gynecological positions to reach them under the bed.

My daring act of rebellion against Blockbuster is paying with a credit card. It costs them much more in fees to the card administrator than the rounding of the change up to a full dollar in cash. I feel sorry for the family behind me in line, for the transaction will take a few seconds longer, but, hey, I'm trying to change the world. One Blockbuster at a time.

If you own or manage a business, be sensible: round it up. Up to 96¢ change, give me a dollar. Better yet, whenever the change ends 6, 7, 8 or 9, round it up to the next nickel. Keep a penny tray on the counter, and you may make up for your "losses" with the coins other clients may leave there.

I have seen businesses obsessed with reconciling their cash registers to the penny at the end of each shift. One fast food company has an anecdotal reputation for firing on the spot the cashiers with differences greater than $10. It would take 250 transactions of 4¢ rounding to make up $10, and it won't happen in one shift. To be realistic, all those cents from rounding up won't make a difference for your business. If you really want to manage your profits, you'll have a greater impact by keeping employees happily motivated to work diligently and efficiently, and by cultivating good relationships with your clients. If you feel that money's going down the drain, improve the management of inventories and waste, with better purchasing practices and frequent physical inventories. If necessary, implement subtle theft-reducing controls, such as buying transparent trash bags and pocketless uniform pants.

I would be very pleased if you priced the most frequently ordered item combinations on your menu to round to a more logical figure after taxes, like $7.75 or $8.00. A round number will allow your cashiers to work more efficiently, reduce transaction time and waiting lines, and might even save you good hard dollars in staffing and wages in the long run.

# Get Them What They Want

A couple of miles from my house, on my way home from work, I witnessed a new restaurant being built almost from scratch, using little of the old building's structure. It was fun to drive by every day during the nine months it took them to complete the construction and see the building advance. It seemed unusual to me that it was an independent restaurant. When I see new construction for a restaurant these days, it's often a chain, because chains are more aggressive with real estate than mom and pops, which often don't have as much budget for construction and generally only do minor modifications to the building. The building was also larger than the average restaurant in the suburbs of Philadelphia, clearly ambitious. The elaborate and ambiguous façade might have been Arabic, Persian, or Aztec. The restaurant name wasn't very telling either, and I wondered what kind of food they would serve. By the amount of time it took them to open, I assumed they had some major legal, licensing, or operational issues, which made me nervous, as someone hoping to eventually have a restaurant of my own.

My first experience there was a trip to the bar. As you entered, contrary to the exotic façade, at first glance it looked very much like an inconspicuous diner: tall booths with colored leather-like plastic upholstery, Formica tables, and bland décor. The refrigerated counter had desserts on display. An additional, more formal and elegant dining room was to one side, a large bar area was to the other. The bar was very successful that Friday night, as it seemed to be most Friday and Saturday nights thereafter when I glanced at the movement when driving by. The crowd was young, and the drinks were flowing. I happily noted their success, but I noticed the relatively empty dining rooms, possibly because it was already a bit late for dinner.

I realized that I still didn't know what kind of restaurant it was. Other than the arabesques on the outside, nothing inside gave me a clue to the theme. No Frank Sinatra on the speakers with photos of huge family meals, no hookahs, no portraits of Indian deities, no Mexican tapestry on the wall. It looked just like a typical American bar attached to an American diner. I left without looking at the dinner menu.

A few weeks later, curiosity overcame me, and I stopped there for lunch with my wife. My timing was a bit unusual, around 3:30 in the afternoon, but it was open and was, again, fairly empty. I looked at the menu, finally discovering that it specialized in Mediterranean cuisine. The selection was ample and interesting, even for a lunch menu. Non-vegetarians would happily find a good selection of fish, poultry, and mollusks, prepared in the typical regional style. They had many options of pasta, but I was in the mood for an eggplant panino. It was well prepared, and so was the ravioli that my wife ordered. We finished with cheesecake and coffee. The price was right, and we were happy.

Weeks later, after a long bicycle ride down the Schuylkill River trail, we invited our tired riding friends for a late brunch there, with the refreshing remark that they serve alcohol. As we arrived, we found a different menu. The name of the restaurant had also changed, and the plates were mostly American comfort food. That suited me, for I quickly and gladly found eggs Benedict and negotiated exchanging half of my plate for a portion of my wife's spinach, mushroom, and cheese omelet. And beer, of course, the foundation of a good brunch.

The meal went well, although we noted that the staff was a bit inexperienced. At a certain point, a couple at a nearby table lost heart waiting for service and left, making clearly known, on their way out, that they were very upset. We were exhausted, our drinks were on the table, and we had no rush whatsoever. When things calmed down, I addressed a woman who seemed frustrated with the staff. "So," I said, "things seemed to have changed from the last time I was here. Has the place been sold already?" This was only a few months after opening, and I was incredulous that the restaurant could have already been sold.

"No, no," she said. "My son-in-law has a successful Mediterranean restaurant in New York and decided to open a similar concept here, moving away from the craziness of the big city life. It seems," she continued, "that the local population wasn't the right clientele for that food. Most people that came in were looking for diner food, so we decided to rename the place and adapt the menu into a diner style."

It could very well be that the building, with two dining areas, each with capacity for seating more than one hundred people, was probably too large for a Mediterranean cafe, and that the population of this area is more traditional in eating habits, but it is also a fact that there are two very successful Mediterranean restaurants within ten miles of my house, where you won't find a table on weekend evenings without a reservation. What seems to be the major issue was that the restaurant they built looked very much like a diner, which messed up expectations. Clients came in expecting eggs, pancakes, steak, and fries, and they surely were confused as they opened the menu and found something dramatically different.

I learned a few things from watching how that restaurant evolved:

- **The shotgun strategy doesn't always work.** They had three ambiences for three entirely different types of clientele: the bar, the casual booths, and the fine dining salon. All in relatively large scales. The concept of different ambiences seems to work for the casual chains, but it didn't match well with the sophistication of the menu. The menu targeted a demographic that wouldn't be seeking bar food, nor were the bar crowds seeking a seafood risotto. They couldn't be everything for everyone, or if they could attract diversity, it would not have been in the scale they wanted; they should have been more specific in defining their target population. The casual dinner and bar crowds were probably the best shot for the area, particularly once they defined that the operation would have such a large scale.

- **You should have a consistent and clear message.** Along my driving route home from another job, a seafood restaurant was clearly named as a seafood restaurant in their original sign. They eventually added a large neon sign saying "Great Steaks." This is crazy! That tells me their seafood sales weren't going well, and they decided to promote beef on their menu. Was the seafood not so good? Would the beef be any better? Would I be interested in checking out either? I drove by recently and found that the restaurant had closed. I have no idea how good it was.

- **You may need to be adaptable, especially after investing a significant amount of money.** The Mediterranean restaurant quickly adapted to what their clientele wanted. True, they confused their clients with the inconsistency in their original concept, but once they started to build a clientele, they agilely served them what they wanted and became successful in their current business. Well done. Of course, adaptation isn't always simple. If you have a seafood restaurant, the only reason you have beef on the menu is to accommodate that person in a party of eight who hates or is allergic to seafood. If you truly believe that beef better suits your clientele, close the restaurant, repaint, rename, and reopen.

I found a nice vegetarian restaurant in the Pocono Mountains area. The owner was a woman of inspiring determination, and the server had the most sincere smile I ever came across. Moreover, the food was delicious. The owner graciously took time to talk to me about the business, investment, and clientele. Their location was very popular among hunters, and she found it impossible to build a solid client base for vegetarian food. Eventually she decided she needed to add fish and poultry to the menu. It broke my heart to see how difficult and painful the decision was for her. Neither she nor I meant to be judgmental of people who serve animal protein, but her need to adapt the menu ran contrary to her original concept and philosophy of life. She respected vegetarians' principles and used separate equipment to cook vegetarian and animal products. Her clientele seemed to be understanding and supportive. Sadly, the story of her restaurant's adaptation was cut short when she lost the battle to a terrible disease, which unmercifully evolved too fast.

One could argue that the Mediterranean café, the seafood place, and the vegetarian restaurant should have conducted more thorough market research before the initial investment. However, finding statistical data on eating habits and preferences for a specific area is extremely difficult, and commissioning a survey is too expensive for the potentially dubious results. People lie about their eating habits, pretending them to be healthier than they actually are. It's also difficult for people to issue a solid opinion based on a conceptual idea of food. This is especially challenging with an unusual restaurant concept, like my plan for a vegetarian restaurant. Potential clients can't reasonably compare my concept to any current operation around the area. I have found solid data indicating that 3 percent of the population in the Northeast is vegetarian, and as much as 12 percent of young women in the United States consider themselves vegetarians. I also found that vegetarian entrées and local sourcing of produce are among the top ten current trends, according to the National Restaurant Association. Although this data encourages me, it isn't specific to my targeted area and demographic. No matter how much data you research and how much common sense you apply, you will have to resign yourself to the fact that, to a certain degree, you won't truly know the demand until you open the doors to the public.

When we see success and failure stories, it's easy to analyze what drove their good or bad performance. But when you talk to independent restaurateurs, they tell you that no matter how good a business plan they had, before they opened, they had no means to predict how many people would actually show up at the door. Adaptability, then, becomes a critical tool that you must learn when and how to use.

I asked a young restaurateur, who bought a failed restaurant nearby, how he turned it around into a profitable business. "Don't be arrogant," he said. "The previous chef-slash-owner was too pretentious. I'm not a chef; I'm a businessman, and I don't have that kind of personal pride. Listen to the clients and serve them what they want. You are not in the business of educating your clients' palates."

# Girl Scout Cookies

The Girl Scout cookies have bothered me for some time now. Not so much for the harassment by co-workers and neighbors, or the barricade of parents with their young daughters at the entrance of every supermarket in Pennsylvania—those, I can understand. As a kid, I sold lots of raffle tickets and collected goodies to be awarded in the festivals of my Catholic school. I understand that the cookies sold by the Girl Scouts help support several charities and the engagement of girls from less privileged families in the Scout activities. In 2008, there were 2.5 million Girl Scouts in the United States, selling more than $17 million in cookies, which represents approximately one-fourth of the revenues that sustain that organization. Looking at their public financial statements, the organization clearly runs in deficit territory and definitely needs to sell a lot of cookies to keep going.

I also know how hard it is for many introverted young girls to break through their shyness and offer their cookies to strangers. I have nothing against the Girl Scouts, and I appreciate their efforts to raise money.

My problem with the Girl Scout cookies is that they are neither fresh, nor baked by the girls. They are industrialized, produced by two large bakeries, one based in Virginia and the other in Kentucky.

The history of the cookies dates back to 1917, when girls and moms baked cookies together in their home kitchens, sold the cookies they made, and directed the money to support the American troops fighting in Europe during World War I and to support the Girl Scout organization itself. I praise the visual image of a young girl and her mom spending time together, learning to cook and bake. And I don't say this to be sexist; they happened to be mostly girls and moms in those days, but I believe that spending time with parents and learning to cook are healthy activities for girls and boys, moms and dads in any permutation. Among other benefits, people who cook from the scratch invariably have better nutrition that those who subsist on TV dinners.

The industrialization of the cookies deconstructs the original concept of child and parent cooking together and bonding in the kitchen, depriving these Scout girls the opportunity to learn to produce food from raw ingredients. It's reflective of a culture of packaged food, which is so detrimental to our health. If I were one of those Girl Scouts nowadays, I would rebelliously fight to bake and sell my own cookies. As a kid, I liked to spend time in the kitchen with my mother and grandmother, and it would have pissed me off to have to sell cookies made by an industrial baker. It might even be that insane governmental sanitation agents drove the Girl Scouts to buy industrial cookies, but, seriously, wouldn't that be worth a national lobbying campaign?

I happen to like some of those cookies, particularly the one with caramel and coconut, but, being industrialized, they are necessarily full of chemical crap. The cookies contain a number of preservatives, stabilizers, artificial flavors, and coloring agents. If the cookies were baked by the girls with their moms, the recipe probably would not include synthetic niacin, thiamin mononitrate and riboflavin, folic acid, high fructose corn syrup, sorbitol, dextrose, glycerine, and artificial colors, all reported on the box's label.

In the restaurant world, a professional kitchen is pressured to serve 150 meals per shift, employing as few as three cooks. Labor is expensive, relative to the prices that an average restaurant can charge its clients. Because kitchens are trimming their staffs, it has become increasingly difficult to find restaurants cooking from fresh ingredients, which requires intensive labor and longer preparation time. As a result, restaurants have become overly dependent on canned vegetables and frozen precooked products. A visit to Restaurant Depot, which is kind of a Costco for restaurant owners, is enough to freak me out. You can find just about anything portioned and pre-cooked.

As with the Girl Scout cookies, I am also frustrated with the industrialization of food in restaurants and the frozen stuff they reheat for service. I don't want to go to an Italian restaurant that serves industrial Alfredo sauce out of a large plastic bag. I want to see you make an effort. At least throw in some fresh ingredients. If you are a true Italian place, why can't you make your own pasta? It's not rocket science. Replace the dried herbs with fresh ones, and use fresh garlic and shallots to flavor your sauce made of canned tomatoes; that's the least you can do to call it "homemade marinara."

I can understand that you may need to use canned artichokes. The cost of fresh ones and the time consumed in preparing them would make prices unpalatable for us, but what justifies canned vegetables such as green beans, carrots, potatoes, or any other vegetable that is inexpensive, readily available, and easy to cook?

As a home consumer, I absolutely despise frozen food, those entrees you just open, heat, and eat. My wife walks through the freezer aisles at the supermarket and sees wonderful boxes of Indian and Thai dishes. Some of these are laborious to prepare at home, and we often don't have all the necessary ethnic ingredients and spices. The beautiful box of Massaman curry vegetables is tempting indeed. Sometimes she buys them; invariably she regrets it. Once you open the box, they don't look anything like the picture, nor do they taste anything like the real deal. So why would I want to go out to eat microwave food in your restaurant? The better use for your freezer is to store frozen fruits and vegetables—which are significantly healthier than their canned versions—or burger patties and meatballs (veggie burger and mushroom "meatballs" for me).

I remember the day my parents got our first microwave. It was a wondrous thing, capable of boiling water in seconds while we stared at the screen. For many years, we all wondered what the use was for that appliance that decorated our kitchen. It wasn't great for cooking. It could make things get very hot, but also very soggy. Most foods heat better in a pan or in a conventional oven. In the pan, you can stir and adjust the moisture and seasoning of the item you are reheating, and the oven gives you that crispiness to your lasagna. One day, a few years later, the purpose of the microwave was finally revealed: popcorn. That is just about the only thing that a microwave oven cooks efficiently. Popcorn pops in three minutes without mess, and the gooey fake butter makes the salt adhere well to every piece of popcorn. Pretty amazing, and delicious too, especially if you refrain from reading the label in search for diacetyl, the chemical responsible for the buttery flavor, which also caused lung disease in factory workers exposed to long periods of inhaling it. Not having popcorn on the menu, a chef who values his dignity will use the microwave for nothing other than reheating his coffee.

Two years ago, I received a vintage stovetop popcorn pan as a birthday gift. It has a rotary device that steers the corn without the need to open the lid or lift the pan from the fire. You gotta keep the air inside the pan very hot for efficient popping, and that pan is designed to prevent any distractions from the heat. My wife and I agree that the old-fashioned popcorn tastes much better, and we have never again bought the microwave packets. My microwave has been lonely. I wonder if any of the Girl Scouts ever had a chance to make stovetop popcorn.

# I May Want Dessert and Coffee

Compared to the restaurant habits in many other countries, here in America, very few people order dessert. The best data I was able to find was published by Technomic, an organization that publishes studies of trends in the restaurant industry. Results vary greatly with restaurant style and dining shift, but the study indicates that 70 percent of Americans order dessert, in average, less than half of the times they dine out. 30 percent of clients hardly ever order dessert.

It could be because we're always in a hurry and don't have the time to spend in a meal with several courses. It may be because the portions for starters, salads, and entrées are enormous, leaving no room for dessert, or that the desserts themselves are disproportionally large for a meal closer. Perhaps it's because the puritans among our settlers taught us not to be forgiving of such indulgences as dessert, and many of us still view sugary treats as a sin. Or maybe it's just because most desserts we find on the menus are boring and predictable, like the banana tempura and vanilla ice cream at Asian restaurants.

I can certainly attest to the fact that at one particular vegan restaurant where I worked, we sold more desserts than at any other restaurant I've ever been to. Their dessert menu was vast, the plating beautiful, and they were tasty. I have no doubt that the creativity and presentation played important factor on the sales.

If you are a server, you should realize that every dessert or coffee your clients order is an additional dollar for you, in tips. As we call it in business, that's low-hanging fruit. Whatever reason prevents more of your clients from ordering desserts, be aware that, provided that the restaurant has good options for dessert, you can motivate the client to order the dessert that he or she probably already wants.

Servers hear a lot about upselling and suggestive selling. Some are better than others on that. Some are shy; others don't believe in it. My first unambiguous observation on the matter was during my culinary school externship, where I was in charge of pizzas, among other things, and every day I had to come up with a pizza special. I had to manage the inventory at my station and take advantage of the grilled vegetables and shitake mushrooms left behind by the lunch crew. But, more importantly, I always made something that I would personally like to eat. Sometimes I heard the servers commenting that the featured pizza looked pretty and exciting. When that happened, the special would be the only pizza I'd be preparing all night and would make it to the

"86 list" before the end of the shift. It proved to me, beyond reasonable doubt, the power the servers have in driving clients' choices. It reinforces the idea that sincerity is a powerful argument. The results are noticeable when servers believe in what they recommend.

Growing up, desserts were a natural and integral part of the meal. To my parents, the idea of a dessert-less meal is inconceivable. Because in America it is culturally less automatic, the server's motivational role is critical. I can't believe I'm actually asking you to try to sell me something, but yes, I am. I usually run from salespeople like my cat runs from children, but possibly because I'm currently more alert to restaurant service practices, it bothers me when servers don't even try to sell me a dessert. Most servers check another box in the mental to-do checklist for every table by asking, "Would you like to take a look at the desserts menu?"

My reaction to that question is "No, thanks. Just the check, please." I'm just conditioned this way and do it without thinking. Also, when you offer for me to look at the desserts menu, it unconsciously suggests there will be incremental effort and delays. You'll find and bring the menu, I'll have to read it, find you again, order, and wait for the dessert. When I do ask to look at the menu, and if I find something interesting, my wife may take a rapid glance at my abdominal area, reminding me that I shouldn't. The waiter, in this case, is my mediator. Rather than an annoying salesperson, you will enable the connection between this chocolate lover and a slice of chocolate cake. You can do this effectively and smoothly.

- If the tables are sufficiently large, leave the desserts menu on the table, preferably at all times. At some point, between drinks or while I'm waiting for my food, I'll look through it. It may make me interested. I'd also prefer to have the full menu always on the table, so I can browse through the options of what I'd order in a future visit. I often feel rushed to make up my mind and order, so I don't always read thoroughly through the options the first time.

- Don't offer me the menu—offer the desserts. As you approach the table, just say, "For desserts, among our offers, our pastry chef prepares a vegan tiramisu that is out of this world; the pecan pie and key lime tart are also very popular."

- Make them smaller. I don't know which came first: the size or the price. But I often see restaurants offering humongous slices of cake for a price equivalent to that of some entrées. Thus, people who already feel guilty for indulging are also faced with a strong monetary reason for declining your offer. I, for one, can assure you that if you cut both by a third, I'll order desserts much more often.

- I've read restaurateurs' comments in trade magazines that bringing dessert trays around the salon is very effective. Visual temptation is more powerful than conceptual temptation. For presentation consistency and sanitary purposes, please use a faux version of your desserts, made of clay and plastic. If you find the cost of commissioning such replicas to be too sinful, try to convince your desserts supplier to foot the bill; they have a vested interest.

- When offering coffees and teas, let us know straight away that you have to-go cups. That will be an incentive if I have a long drive or if we're going back to the office, where the coffee tastes like an ashtray wash.

- For Pete's sake, brew some decent coffee. It's a matter of pennies per cup to upgrade to premium coffee beans. If your coffee is as bad as that at the office, I probably won't order yours again in the future, opting for the bad coffee that I can get for free. Even at restaurants that specialize in brunches, the coffee is often terrible. How can you possibly neglect the quality of your coffee if you're serving breakfast?

There's no better example of a win/win negotiation than one where I get the dessert I wanted, but was reluctant to order, the restaurant makes more profits and the wait staff get more tips. Sometimes you'll be successful, sometimes not, but a good salesperson will tell you that you have to follow every lead and believe in every opportunity. Without pushing too hard, give a try at making us excited about your desserts. Offering the menu is not enough.

# Reputation

While at some cooking schools you can barter the food you prepared food with that of the neighboring kitchens, at ours, each class ate what they cooked, which was a good opportunity for us to evaluate the quality of our products, listen to chef's critique, and make our own judgments.

At the end of one class of Asian cuisine, we had produced some fifteen different dishes, and I tried a bit of everything. I was particularly curious about some Vietnamese potato pancakes, which seemed to have a nice twist to the latkes and hash browns we usually eat. The pancakes looked nice, golden brown, not too greasy, nicely shaped into two-inch circles. I dipped one in a ginger sauce and took a bite. Something didn't feel right, a little too hard and with a bad crunch. It was a whole dried peppercorn; bitter, spicy, and not the taste I was looking for. I mentioned it to one guy at my table, and, further dissecting the little pancakes in my plate, I found a few more whole peppercorns. Those are not something you serve unless you are specifically cooking steak au poivre, when you should be using fresh peppercorns.

The guy at my table shouts:

—Yo, who made the potato pancakes?

—"I did," someone responds from another table.

—Dude, there's like whole peppercorns in there!

—I know; I tried to crush them with the knife, but they were too hard and wouldn't break, so I said fuck it and threw the whole thing in there.

"Fuck it," I whined. That's right, fuck the client—I assumed that was his attitude at the restaurant where the kid was a line cook after classes.

"Wanna eat nicely crushed pepper, go somewhere else, 'cause that ain't what we serve here!"

That was not the first time I had seen cooks act this way: "Fuck it" when rinsing dirt off leaves, deveining shrimp, cleaning a station, or wearing gloves when working with finished products. There are lots of lazy slobs out there.

If the temptation for this attitude ever crosses your mind, I need to tell you this: people are watching. All the time. Your reputation is built every day, every minute. If one day, one of us from that class were in a position to hire or refer the peppercorn guy, some of us probably wouldn't endorse him. I wouldn't and I barely know him. I only took that one class with that group, but I know him as the guy who wouldn't take a few steps to the grinder (if the peppercorns were too tough for his knife) and do what he was supposed to do not to ruin his food. The food you plate is your representation of self. Your food is your business card, your Facebook page. It's how the world sees you, and we clients may not have any other background information to give context, as we form an impression of you. One little peppercorn incident, and you may lose all respect and credibility you might have had with me.

I saw a few things during my corporate days. I witnessed jerky managers pay the price for mistreating their employees. People reap what they sow; sooner or later, things eventually catch up with them. We had a manager who loved to expose everybody else to save his ass, using very malleable versions of the truth. Among other evildoings, he would routinely and deliberately wait until the very last minute to ask us to prepare information, and then tell his boss that he couldn't meet the deadline because we were late, naming each one of us. When our manager was placed under a new boss, who didn't like him very much, we threw him in the fire, providing many detailed accounts of our manager's incompetence and lack of integrity, lobbying tirelessly that he should go. The man was fired a few months later. He was the only person in all my professional years that I actually came to hate.

I've also contributed to the decisions of promoting or laying off a number of people, both below and above my rank. In such times, we tried to be as comprehensive and fair as possible, by gathering all the data available on their performances, but it's undeniable that the subjective perception that each of us has of our colleagues, subordinates, and managers is a very critical factor.

Not meaning to sound like your fifth-grade teacher, I must say this: always try to do things as best as you can, all the time. It will make a difference in the long run, when building up your personal reputation.

If you are a manager or a business owner, you should know that the devil may indeed be in the details. Even if your budget is limited, neat cuts on your vegetables, balanced seasoning in your sauce, nice diamond grill markings on your meat, or a clean presentation of your plate can set you apart from your competition without impacting your food costs. The clients will notice how you care for your food.

If you go around saying "Oh, fuck it" very often, like the kid with the peppercorns, it will contaminate your business's reputation.

# Bread and Circus

The Roman Empire reached the apex in dominance and wealth during the second century AD, extending from Egypt to Brittany. Those days of prosperity were also marked by relative political stability, teaching us that then, as now, institutional solidity and economic success are powerful complementary factors.

This period of fortune had been preceded by more troublesome times for the rulers of the Empire, when replacement of leadership was done with pragmatism. In the year 44 BC, Julius Caesar frustrated the senators with his disregard for term limits as the Republic's Consul, and his choice for the self-proclaimed title of Perpetual Dictator. He was assassinated on the Senate's floor, in a plot led by Brutus, suspected to be Caesar's bastard son. In 30 BC, Mark Antony, a loyal friend of Julius Caesar and one of the three men who governed the Roman republic after Caesar's death, found himself under siege by forces led by another governor, Octavius, and committed suicide.

Octavius, later named Augustus, eventually centralized ruling power and is generally regarded as Rome's first emperor. When very ill, Augustus chose Postumus Agrippa to be his heir for the throne, but Agrippa was assassinated before having a chance to claim power. The Senate chose Augustus' stepson, Tiberius, to succeed him, but after the assassination of his own son, Tiberius decided to exile himself from Rome and reportedly lived in constant paranoia until his death, which some historians believe to have been commissioned by Caligula, one of the two men Tiberius had appointed to govern after his passing. Caligula quickly had Tiberius's grandson assassinated, to remove the competition. Caligula himself was killed in 41 AD and succeeded by Claudius, who was presumably poisoned to death in the year 54 AD. Nero, Claudius' great-nephew and appointed successor, might have participated in the assassination. Nero, of course, is famously accused of having set Rome on fire in an alleged attempt to clear an area to build a palatial complex. Surrounded by rebel forces opposed to Rome's tax policies, Nero put an end to his own life in 68 AD. Only the third emperor after Nero died of natural causes.

Overstretched in their vast dominance, the empire's army battled on too many fronts, eventually succumbing in the fifth century, dilapidated by the forces of rebellious groups like the Visigoths and Germanic tribes, and weakened by the rise of other regional empires, like the Huns and Persians.

The poet Juvenal, a cynical satirist of the first century, wrote about the obliviousness of the people to the absurdities of their governors. In *Satire 10*, he portrayed the formerly idealistic Roman people as resigned to lazy contentment, supporting brutal and corrupt governments as long as they were appeased with *panem et circenses*—bread and circus.

It's been a caricature of many populist leaders in modern history that their success in attaining and retaining power lies in keeping people's basic needs fed and their minds distracted. Dictators in Africa take a more literal route, controlling the food distribution—including humanitarian assistance—and promoting soccer tournaments and other sorts of entertainment to take the edge off the hardships faced by the population. Or they may chose other means of distracting public attention, directing anger and revolt to a minority tribe, making them seemingly culpable for the social illnesses of the country.

In a less grim setting, "bread and circus" are exactly we expect to find in a restaurant. We will overlook some idiosyncrasies of your concept and minor operational imperfections if good food comes out of the kitchen and we have a good time in the dining room.

The entertainment component usually relates to the proverbial ambience. Good company and a nicely composed décor will suffice to please our minds, but if you go to a hibachi grill, the circus is more evident. I don't mean "circus" in a demeaning manner; many people enjoy the fantasy of escaping to Australia or to a tropical forest for an evening meal. And it can be quite amusing to watch a skillful sushi master making precise agile cuts with his Kasumi knife, a pizzaiolo spinning pizza dough in the air, or an executive chef plating a gorgeous dish.

One morning, we had a class demonstration by our dean of culinary arts, Chef Hunt. He is an elegant man of many resources, who's notably been through every corner of a restaurant. His movements are polished and smooth, as someone who'll never look clumsy in front of his audience. He showed us the classical preparation of crepes Suzette. Once upon a time, the fire marshal would allow the tableside preparation of such dessert, with abundant amounts of cognac and Grand Marnier. You cannot avoid being amazed while staring at the three-foot-tall flames caramelizing the sugar and building a crispy crust to the crêpe. But you don't need quite as much pyrotechnics to look skillful or entertaining. Chef Hunt served us the crepes working a fork and a spoon between his fingers like they were tongs, as many old-time waiters do. "Holding the utensils like this," he said, "is a simple thing, but looks a little different from what people do at home. When people come to restaurants, they like to see something different."

As an owner, cook, server, bus person, host, or manager, try to do something different. Amuse us. Not every bartender can juggle with five bottles, but anyone can learn a couple of tricks, such as separating colors of liquids of different density or developing an elegant way of pouring Scotch, perhaps inducing us into believing we're getting a more generous serving.

I found it intriguing the first time I saw a waiter write his name upside down on the paper mat. I'm now ready to see a few new tricks.

In Philadelphia, there is a restaurant where the servers sing arias of famous operas. There, they do make sure that the servers they hire can actually sing; virtually all of them are music students at good universities. Be sensible about what tricks you perform. Roman emperors routinely ordered poor performers to be beheaded.

# Vegetarians

I have been a vegetarian for seven years. My cholesterol once climbed to over 250, and my family history of coronary problems is a concern to be taken seriously. My genetic heritage drives my body to produce quite a lot of cholesterol, so I'm not required to eat any of it. Cholesterol is critical in keeping the right structure and flexibility of our cells' membranes, not too hard and not too soft. The excess of "bad" cholesterol in our blood, however, oxidizes when in contact with free radicals of oxygen, which result from our regular metabolism. When oxidized, this "bad" cholesterol, LDL, damages the walls of blood vessels and accumulates on these scratched walls, along with other solid particles from your blood, causing further inflammation and buildup. The formation of this plaque ultimately hardens and narrows the interior of arteries, possibly leading to strokes, heart attacks, or thrombosis. Maintaining a low level of cholesterol can retard this process to a point that you may die very old or from a different cause.

Animal products, except for seafood, contain cholesterol in abundance, hence the urge for me to avoid them. Not eating fish was, for me, more of a philosophical choice than a health one. Various fish offer generous amounts of omega-3 fatty acids, proven to be an important nutritional component, which contributes to children's growth and the maintenance of healthy neurological functions. Omega 3 is also believed to prevent the oxidation of LDL cholesterol. These fatty acids are also found in several vegetables, being particularly plentiful in flaxseed and walnuts. Despite some potential bad stuff found in the waters where fish dwell, like mercury and pollution-borne pathogens and toxins, you may conclude that, overall, eating fish is healthy for you, although not so much for the fish.

A well-balanced omnivorous diet, as well stated in *In Defense of Food*, by Michael Pollan, might prove to be as healthy as being vegetarian, as long as you eat a diverse spread of plants as the overwhelming majority of your diet. I initially chose to become vegetarian for nutritional reasons. Gradually, I gained other motives for my decision: the growth hormones and antibiotics fed to cattle and poultry, the cruelty under which livestock is often raised, the unnecessary slaughter of a complex organism to satisfy my appetite, when a wide variety of vegetables and vegetable-based products are broadly available and suffice for complete nutrition, my interest in Buddhism, and the fact that meats are messier, smellier, and potentially more time consuming to prepare and clean.

I effortlessly reduced my consumption of meats, only eating beef, poultry, or fish when I ate out. One day, after the gastronomical insanities of a holiday season, I decided I would give vegetarianism a go. I found, to my dismay, that it is quite possible not to lose weight while being vegetarian, as long as I kept eating too much and made sure to include lots of cheese and carbs. Despite my waistline's reluctance to recede, replacing meats with vegetables produced blood screening results that made my doctor smile.

I also found that being vegetarian somehow offends certain people, even though I am not a very vocal activist of the cause and I don't go around evangelizing people or pretending to be superior to anyone because of my eating habits. I learned my lesson one day, long before I chose to be vegetarian, when I was talking about bullfights with Craig, a vegetarian friend, and how I found them cruel. "Well," he said, "those bulls are raised in large pastures and fed well, and at least they have a chance of surviving in the arena, as low as the odds may be. These bulls will fight only once. If they survive, they will be used for breeding. A little hypocritical, isn't it, that you're willing to eat meat, but can't stand seeing an animal be killed?" Point taken. I've since been mindful of what I say about the issue.

Every so often, someone, finding about my eating habits, will seek to have a discussion on the topic, and I will have to deal with the strangest questions regarding vegetarianism. Many of the vegetarians I know go through the same, so here are a few answers to help you better understand your vegetarian clients, we weird creatures:

- No, fish is not a vegetable. Neither is chicken.

- Some vegetarians dislike the taste or texture of meat, or their body doesn't react well to it. That is not my case. But whatever reason someone has for preferring to not eat meat, I don't see why their reasoning must be qualified and judged to an arbitrary scale of authenticity and respectability. People have refused to try my eggplant, and my ego survived the experience intact. Please don't take it as a personal offense when we turn down your barbecue ribs.

- No, I won't die if I eat meat. If I am in someone's house, whose grandmother took the time and trouble to cook a meal for me and unadvisedly used meat in it, I may, politely, eat some, but

I would focus on the vegetarian side dishes. I'm not obliged to be vegetarian; I simply choose and prefer to eat vegetarian.

- Yes, some vegetarians are tempted by sushi, bacon, fried chicken, or a slice of New York strip. They might succumb to such temptation, every so often. Does that make them fake-vegetarians or hypocrites? Why should a vegetarian be held to such high standards of faultlessness no other group of people is expected to attain?

- Some vegetarians eat dairy products, either because they enjoy milk and cheese, or because they believe it's a necessary source of calcium. Cows need not be killed for us to get milk, which explains why dairy is philosophically acceptable for these veg-etarians. However, most cattle are raised cruelly, which moti-vates a large number of vegetarians to completely avoid dairy, or choose milk from pasture-roaming cows, where more hu-mane farming and improved nutrition are found. Read Michael Pollan, and you'll have a detailed explanation why their milk, as well as the cage-free hens' eggs, contain better nutrition. Roaming animals have a diet more suitable for their digestive systems. Cows eat more leaves instead of the grains and ani-mal byproducts fed to confined cattle, resulting in healthier animals and more nutritious milk, while avoiding the cruelty of confinement. Due to her objection to the practice of keeping cows in a continuous cycle of pregnancy followed by separa-tion from the calves, to produce milk for our consumption, my wife has switched to coconut milk, and that's what you'll find in my fridge.

- About 99.7% percent of eggs are unfertilized, so eating eggs doesn't kill a chick embryo. If you saw what standard chicken cages look like, you would realize there's no room for romance. As an egg-eater, I'm not a hypocrite for killing an embryo, be-cause there is no embryo; I'm a hypocrite because I shouldn't endorse the cruelty exercised by the egg industry. I now buy free-range hens' eggs, which allows for slightly less cruelty to those animals, but I would be more consistent with my prin-ciples if I were a full-time vegan. I'm working on it.

- I understand that humans are omnivorous as a result of five million years of evolution. Note, however, that evolution doesn't care if you die of a heart attack at thirty-five or cancer at fifty, as long as you reproduce before you die. Also bear in mind that the amazing availability of diverse vegetables for our consumption is a recent event. Not too long ago, meats were a nutritional necessity within regions that could only produce potatoes, beets, and cabbages during short seasonal periods. Now, without breaking a sweat, you can find in your supermarket all the essential amino acids, vitamins, and minerals you need to be a healthy human being, all within the aisles of plant-based foods.

- Plants suffer too, you say. Okay, so let's assume, although without much credible scientific support, that plants might possibly have feelings. Do you truly believe that the neurological system in a lettuce equals the one in a pig? Do you contend that the confinement and slaughtering of a cow compares to the growing and picking of a carrot? If that's your counterargument to vegetarianism, just... go fuck yourself. I'm sorry; I can't even begin to argue with that logic, or lack thereof.

The disdain for vegetarians is evident in most menus. Too many restaurants do not offer anything vegetarian. Zippo, nada. Mind you, vegetarians have very low expectations of the options they will find when dining out and will be satisfied with little. Vegans have no expectations at all of finding anything suitable for their preferences within the entrées, and will settle for a salad or a combination of sides.

One common issue I must also clarify is that we don't choose to go to a steakhouse. Either we join a group of carnivore friends, or it's the only viable restaurant within a distance. All we want is one option of appetizer (onion rings, fried zucchini fingers); a soup (black beans, cream of broccoli); and an entrée (gnocchi pomodoro, roasted vegetables and tofu, stuffed peppers). Nothing too fancy, just one option, so we don't have to give full explanations of our food "orientation" to the server and request the chef to assemble something special.

To my complete disappointment, I learned at cooking school that many of the items I assumed to be vegetarian are cooked with meat products. Beans, rice, and vegetable soups are often cooked with chicken stock. Eggplant is often breaded with the same Panko crumbs that was previously used for breading chicken breasts, and Portobello caps are grilled among bloody burgers. And whose idea was it to sprinkle bits of bacon over sides of broccoli and potato salad?

As much as four percent of the American population consider themselves vegetarian. Discounting those who regularly eat white meats and would be better classified as Flexitarians, the statistic settles at approximately two percent. You may want to consider that two percent is a sizable portion of the restaurant public, and the percentage of vegetarians is greater in the more educated and affluent segments of society. Please keep us in mind as you design your menu, and please indicate clearly on the menu when foods are vegetarian or, at least, clarify the servers on the preparation and ingredients of the foods. They should know it anyway, for dealing with questions related to food allergies.

If you chose a vegan recipe for your one vegetarian item on the menu, you'll be pleasing vegans and lacto-ovo vegetarians alike.

Other types of vegetarians choose more selective diets, like those who only eat raw vegetables—raw vegetarians—or ripe fruits fallen from trees—fruitarians—but, frankly, such people are so food-conscious that they probably also seek locally farmed organic produce, no refined grains or sugars, low sodium content in the preparation, and no preservatives or artificial additives. They will likely not enter your restaurant unless you specifically cater to them. If they do come in, they'll probably order a salad with dressing on the side and hope that you don't mess that up.

A recent movement called Meatless Mondays is picking up popularity in some regions of the country. Maybe if you incorporate it into your concept, you could have some success in filling more tables on that slow day of the week and stimulate the chefs' creativity for adding vegetarian dishes to the permanent menu.

# Children First

Sigmund Freud explained that birth is very traumatic for a baby. At that moment, you are suddenly deprived of the warmth, the constant availability of food, and the overall comfort of the womb, and exposed to a cold, dry, and inhospitable delivery room. You may find it challenging to believe that hanging upside down and tightly immersed in liquid was an enjoyable experience, but your mother was your own luxury cruise ship. Thus, he explains, the child has difficulty adapting to the new limitations in comfort and must learn to identify herself as an individual, instead of part of the contained system in which the child once lived. The process of breaking motherly ties and of understanding limits to our wish fulfillment has many steps, which are the most critical events that will define our personalities.

In early childhood, we gradually learn to discern sensations of discomfort, as if the "check engine" light keeps going on and we don't quite know what to do with that information. It takes time for children to understand what it is that is bothering them and how to express it, so they call for attention and ask adults to help them figure out what to do.

When children come to restaurants, they often experience lots of latent energy contained in reduced activity levels, as well as various types of discomfort: cold, hunger, boredom, sleepiness, or an uncomfortable wet diaper. If you are lucky, discomfort will alternate with some periods of distracted introspection and quietness.

When children come to your restaurant, you want to minimize discomfort and maximize the periods of tranquility:

- Bring them bread as quickly as possible. Bread goes a long way with children.

- Having available toys helps, but toys intended to be returned at the end of the meal are a sanitary problem. Toys invariably visit children's mouths, where all kinds of bacteria and viruses dwell. If you also rub the toy with a bit of dairy mac and cheese sauce, you have excellent conditions for a bacterial culture. Also be mindful that many toys, like most things in children's hands, could be harmful, and you don't want to be liable for having allowed little Jane to swallow the airplane's propeller. I would recommend a single-use box of crayons along with a pad to draw on or a coloring book. Then, please, don't mess with the play! I once saw a waiter take the crayon from a boy's hand to write his name on the paper tablecloth. Matt was playing with the brown crayon, and the server had decided that he needed a dark crayon. That didn't go well, and the waiter had a tough time approaching the table thereafter.

- Actors have a saying that children and pets are nightmares for live performances. You simply don't know how children will react, for they are still learning our rules of politeness and civility. To stay on the safe side, don't try to play with them, and remember that some parents are paranoid with strangers getting close or, heaven forbid, patting, hugging, kissing, or touching their children even in the most innocent way. Save yourself from potential grief, and refrain from squeezing those lovely cheeks.

- Bring their food first, ahead of their parents'—immediately, if possible. At least one of the parents will not be able to eat while he or she feeds their young ones, and most adults prefer to eat their food hot. By bringing the children's food first, you will allow parents to better enjoy their own meals later.

- Have something on the menu adequate for infants in size and palate. In most restaurants, parents have to choose between ordering appetizers or cannibalizing their own plates to feed the children. In addition, grown-up foods aren't always suitable or may not be appreciated. With their taste buds in development, children have narrower comfort zones and are sensitive to strong flavors. Children in India, for example, can be very fond of spicy curry dishes, but most children here aren't used to screaming hot chilies. But don't just offer junk on the children's menu. Give a chance to parents who try to feed their children healthier choices and offer children healthier options more diverse and interesting than mac and cheese and chicken nuggets.

# Babette's Feast

It was a strange New Year's holiday. It was a bad time for me professionally, and I had been dumped by a girlfriend who had also left town for good, burning my last thread of hope of getting back together. With moderate expectation of cheering up, I joined my friends, five couples, on a holiday trip, as we often did at that time of the year to spend time together.

The hotel was set up like a villa and seemed dramatically better in the ad photos than in real life. It announced horses for riding and a squash court, but the horses looked sad and ill and made the squash court their private bathroom.

During our first lunch together, Vince announced, in the most awkward possible way, that his new girlfriend, who we were meeting that trip, was pregnant, creating a fantastic level of discomfort at the table and leaving astonished mute faces scrambling for a reaction. After a moment of shock, we offered many congratulations.

Later that day, I went back to my room for a lonely afternoon nap. As I was just dozing off, getting some well-earned rest and taking my mind away from my torments, I heard bizarre music coming through the window: a quasi-star, host of a children's show on our public television, had taken her acoustic guitar to the courtyard outside my room to sing songs about the frog and the grasshopper to her children, making sleep an impossibility for me. A little groggy, I went out to find the guys coming back from a soccer game. In a rough dispute, one of them had been pushed against the goal's pole and broke a rib. We marched to the hospital and spent the good portion of the first night of our trip there.

The next couple of days passed uneventfully. The weather was too cold for us to use the swimming pool, we chose not to play any more soccer, and we spent our time playing snooker and drinking beer in the intervals of counseling one of the couples through their cycle of breaking up and getting back together. New Year's Eve was boring, and I didn't have a midnight kiss.

As we left on January 1, one of the girls mentioned she had heard about a nice Russian restaurant in a nearby town, and we decided to check it out. It was run by a lovely couple, with a cozy ambience you will only find in the most special of bed and breakfasts. Owners and employees still seemed a bit sore from the big celebration service the previous night. We were seated in a small room, similar to many other rooms around the house, where eleven people could have comfort and privacy. Our group is often noisy; privacy suits us well. The restaurant served a tasting menu with a few choices of main course. The owner offered us homemade vodka served in ten-ounce bottles on blocks of ice. He explained, among many other stories, the toasting rituals in Russia at the times of Czar Peter the Great. It was rude, he said, when toasting to Peter, to leave any residue of vodka in the shot glass. We took many in the name of Peter, until we finally finished their homemade vodka inventory, literally.

His wife and two assistants brought an exquisite and endless parade of dishes: caviar canapés, salmon mousse, herring, borsht, pierogies, shrimp crepes, eggplant soufflé, meat pastries, Pojarski, Podjarka, chicken Kiev, and finally a delicious creamy dessert made with Swiss chocolate, which left us speechless, but very *mmming*.

The small-kitchen pace of service was just right for a holiday afternoon. Enough time to savor each course carefully and have a few sips in between. We received every dish with standing ovation, in part because they were that good, and in part as a side effect of our libations to the great Russian ruler (who, after brief research later, we found to be quite a controversial figure; flamboyant in his early life, modernizer of Russia's government and society, and promoter of education, while also an enthusiast of bellicose tyranny with some fondness for torture). Peter was praised by many in the bourgeoisie, and later generally regarded as the manifestation of evil on earth by the Russian Bolsheviks.

The afternoon was one of pure joy and pleasure, as a banquet feast should be. We ate like kings, laughed, and lifted our spirits. We bonded once more as the happy family of friends we are, in some of the best three hours we've ever spent together. What an unexpectedly cheerful way we had found to begin the year.

From time to time, during the meal, one of us would have a synapse of reality and mention, "Man, this is really much better that I expected it to be. Does anybody have any idea how much the fixed-price menu costs?" None of us had the forethought of asking beforehand. By that time it was too late, and at that point, no one really wanted to find it out. Facing the inevitable, we relaxed and enjoyed our meal. If one of us would have to sell a kidney to settle the bill, so be it. Once the check came, we feared opening the folder and kept passing it along around the table. Alice, the lawyer among us, took the initiative, as usual. After a few moments of suspense, she calculated the split at $42 per person. Some of us sighed in relief; others rushed to recalculate, for it couldn't possibly be correct.

We've been there a few other times, and the food quality has never dropped. I'm not sure the owners have matched my current group of almost middle-age folks to the thunderous young group who once drank all the booze and gave standing applause to every course, the guys who took many pictures with him, his wife, and his employees. That restaurant is one of those places that make us happy for the plain fact that it exists, and I hope the owners have a sense of how much they are appreciated. I also hope they forgave Chang for having had issues handling all the vodka he drank that day and the mess he made on his failed rush to embrace the toilet.

The restaurant doesn't follow current standards of expediency for turning tables quickly: service and seating are slow. It doesn't allow for too many table turnings, but the preset tasting menu keeps the kitchen operation simple and controlled. The restaurant is still active, and the menu still costs about $30 per person. They continue to be successful.

I learned that fantastic food at reasonable prices is itself a heck of an attraction, enough to make us drive two hours just for a meal. The simple service dispenses with the hot hostess and the maitre d' in tuxedo, while still being warm and personal. The owner has always greeted us at the door, walked us through rooms filled with Russian and Ottoman objects, and told the stories of how they came to acquire them. The plates take their time to arrive at our table, but it never makes us anxious. I've learned that service doesn't need to be fancy: a setting that looks like a grandmother's house, hosted by pleasant people who serve delicious food, has an aura of authenticity and integrity. That restaurant has made us feel at home and have the time of our lives, giving us a lifetime of memories.

# For My Dog

Where I come from, people are embarrassed to take home their unfinished food. They fear being looked upon with the discomfort we feel when seeing homeless people picking food from the trash. In America, however, wrapping up the leftovers is a casual and usual practice. I believe it's a combination of people being more open about money consciousness, of servings being larger here than anywhere else in the world, and of Americans, on average, not cooking much at home.

The expression "doggy bag" doesn't exist in Portuguese; Americans coined it for the inhibited pretense that the leftover food was being taken to feed the dog. Nowadays, I rarely hear it used, for there's no need to pretend. Everybody takes food home. It's the only way I can leave room for dessert at the Cheesecake Factory and not feel sorry for leaving so much food on the plate. I'm not leaving without having my favorite chocolate cheesecake. It's also another opportunity for your clients to enjoy your restaurant, at their next meal at home.

Overall, servers are good at offering to "wrap it up," and I have never gotten a bad face when I asked to take leftovers home. What's often sad is the presentation. By the time I get home, it's all mushed together, looking like a sad chunk of goo. When I unpack it, it doesn't look appetizing at all. What was I thinking? I didn't want to throw it away, but now I have to eat this? If only grandma were here. She could turn absolutely any leftover food into a ball that would be delicious after deep frying. My wife, I'm afraid, won't let me use my deep fryer except for very special occasions, like the Super Bowl snacks.

I believe it would be nice of you to make packed leftover foods look as appealing as possible, for it's a reminder of the quality of your restaurant. If there's a full piece of grilled tofu, but the mashed potatoes are all messy, maybe you could put a fresh scoop of mashed potatoes on my container. If there's no sauce left on the plate, maybe another one-ounce ladle of sauce will make it more presentable. When the client opens it at home, it will remind her of how nice it was at the restaurant. Product strategists call it "reassurance marketing," as in those labels inside some appliances and electronics boxes: "Congratulations for buying this Nokia" or "It's a Sony." It reassures the customer that the money was well spent, when he might be regretting not buying the cheaper brand. The dog I don't have would love a neat presentation of the leftovers.

One note of caution: there have been contamination issues with leftovers, because clients overlook the four-hour maximum limit for prepared foods to be exposed to the temperature danger zone, the range between 41 and 135 degrees Fahrenheit, in which bacteria grows faster. Once the food leaves your restaurant, you'll have no control over its care, but a sick client may deem you to be at fault and seek compensation. You might want to label your containers with information on proper transportation, storage, refrigeration, reheating procedures, and use-by date.

# Pride and Prejudice

A few months ago, I read a story about a fairly fancy restaurant in New York that offered a chicken sandwich for lunch. Being one of the leanest items on the menu, it attracted the attention of people trying to manage their weight. The sandwich contained aioli, a garlic mayonnaise.

A client ordered the sandwich without the dressing, and the well-informed server explained that the sandwich would be very dry and that it would probably not be a good choice. The client insisted, got what he asked for, took a couple of bites, and sent it back, saying it was the worst sandwich ever made in Manhattan. Over a period, the dryness complaint reoccurred with a few other clients who also requested the sandwich without mayo, until the chef decided that from then on there would be absolutely no substitutions to the menu. I recalled this story last weekend, as a friend was telling me of an instance when she, pregnant, ordered a lobster ravioli, and the restaurant wouldn't give her Parmesan cheese to sprinkle on top of it, under any circumstances. The chef designed the plate without cheese and didn't want the lobster flavor spoiled by an ignorant client used to dumping Parmesan on her spaghetti. The servers had been instructed to not even bother going back to the kitchen to ask for cheese; the answer would always be "No." Fannie, empowered by her pregnancy—who wants to fight with a pregnant woman?—sent the ravioli back to the kitchen and ordered something else.

So a few cooks and I debated these two cases and, after careful pondering and analysis, we came to a unanimous conclusion: the hell with the chef! Seriously, take your pride and shove it up, together with the cheese grater.

In the real world, differently from the chef's conceptual utopia, people traditionally dip their fries in ketchup, have syrup on their pancakes, and sprinkle some Parmesan on their pasta. And if the chicken sandwich is one of the few lean options on the menu, you'd better expect people to request no mayo.

The problem with this picture is the chef, who may or may not have anticipated people's reactions, but decided that she would, if necessary, reeducate her clients' habits to protect the integrity of her food. My reaction when you try to impose stuff on me is not favorable to you ever seeing me again. My friend is more confrontational and made sure to state her case: that she was going to have her food as she wanted it or she wouldn't have it at all.

So, what should you do if your chef doesn't want cheese to interfere with the seafood flavor, relies on mayo for moisture, or makes specially seasoned potato fries that shouldn't dive into ketchup? Here's the question you must first answer: are you one of the fifty restaurants in the entire world that are innovative and special enough that your clients willingly submit blindly to the food experiences as you intend them? If you aren't Per Se, Noma or L'Arpège, you have no business pissing off people by saying no to reasonable requests. I understand your point; I too don't like it when people refuse some ingredient on the plate I prepared, conflicting with my vision of what the composition should be, and it does bother me when people pour ketchup on a finely prepared pizza. I hear you, point noted, but your chef is wrong. More importantly, his reaction is wrong: taking offense and establishing an inflexible policy.

You should look at the situation as an opportunity. It seems that people are interested in the chicken sandwich, but some are reluctant about the mayo, so can I use something else? A white bean spread, maybe? Some light creamy dressing? A vegetable coulis? What about the lobster ravioli? Maybe a grated white cheese that is lighter in flavor and won't interfere with the seafood? For the potatoes, make your own ketchup or dip, complementing the seasoning on the fries. Serve that stuff on the side; let your clients decide.

Why would you want to fight your clients? Is it worth it? Can you afford to do it in the long run?

While we're on this topic, let me make this request one more time: please leave salt shakers on *all* the tables. I don't care about your pride and, as long as my blood pressure is around 120/80, I will season my food with the amount of salt I like. Well, almost as much as I like; my wife will stop me halfway through.

# Something Strange in My Salad

I hate very few foods. One of the items I absolutely loathe is fennel. It has that bittersweet taste of anise, which my palate finds very offensive. I will never, knowingly, order anything containing fennel, with the exception of grilled vegetables previously marinated with a few fennel seeds amongst other spices.

My request for you is simple: disclose on the menu any particularly pungent or often-disliked items in a dish. Mushrooms, beans, eggplant, sauerkraut, horseradish, jalapeños, and strong or hot spices are a few examples of foods I've seen rejected with some frequency. In addition, if you truly believe that fennel is necessary to harmonize your salad, please don't mince it. If you do, I won't be able to set it apart on my plate, and I will struggle to eat your salad. In salads, you often want the client to witness and enjoy the beauty of the fresh leaves, vegetables, and garnishes, and identify each one of them. Quality red leaf lettuce and ripe Cherokee Purple tomatoes are expensive. You want to show them off in larger cuts, instead of tearing and mincing them into minuscule indistinguishable bits. If you make composed salads with brunoise-diced ingredients, like the works of art they serve at a vegan restaurant in Philadelphia, choose mildly-flavored ingredients, as that excellent restaurant did.

You may have thought that this chapter would be about strange creatures in the food. Well, why not? Let's address that too. Now that I better understand the supply chain and all the steps food must take from the crop fields to my plate, I must say: shit happens. In fact, it happens quite a lot. I've read it both on *National Geographic* and the *Wall Street Journal*, so I'll assume they thoroughly checked the story, that we inadvertently eat, on average, one pound of insects each year. Yikes! So much for being vegetarian, eh? Gazillions of flies, bees, ants, and grasshoppers, happily and distractedly munching on kernels of wheat or corn, meet their fate by being squeezed, ground, milled, or roasted along with the plants, seeds, and grains that form the base of most of our foods.

As a customer, I now acknowledge that many creatures of nature are present at plantations, warehouses, and along the roads through which crates of tomatoes travel, that restaurants' salads are rushed at the salad station, often run by only one person, and that sometimes this person trusts the information on the package, which states that the leaves are pre-rinsed and ready to serve. Even if these leaves were packed immaculately clean and one hundred percent bug-free—which they aren't—can the storage and service areas realistically be kept 100% free of bugs? One bug climbs onto a case of mushrooms between the truck and the walk-in fridge, and you have a loose creature roaming among your food. While it's worrisome that a giant cockroach would reach my table unnoticed on the plate, it is understandable that, once in a while, a small leaf-eater worm or a fruit fly may pass the screening. The situation is unpleasant, but it's not the end of the world, nor does it indicate that the kitchen is filthy. I would give the restaurant the benefit of the doubt, return the salad, and ask for something else without much alarm.

On the first instance I find an object on my plate that doesn't belong, I'll likewise assume it was an accident. Despite the good precautions you take when sorting through your ingredients, wearing headgear that prevents hair from falling into the food, and making sure you have no loose jewelry that could dive into a pan of soup, a risk always remains that a sticker that was glued to the tomato or a piece of plastic accidentally sliced with the cheese could find its way to my plate. Even so, if it happens too often, your clients will scatter.

All I ask of you are good sanitation practices. If your storage is clean and the work area is neat, these events will be rare, and the only thing I'll be picking from the salad is the fennel.

For us clients, the saying goes that finding a bug on the plate halfway through the meal is much better than finding half of the bug at the end of the meal.

# This Thing Is Not Hollandaise Sauce

One of my challenges in giving up eggs and dairy is that I love eggs Benedict. Eggs Florentine, in my case. One account of the origin of this dish dates back to the 19th century, when a regular client asked the chef at Delmonico's in New York—yes, the same place that gave us the "86" jargon—to come up with something different. The chef, it seems, reacted quickly, with the ingredients at hand in Delmonico's classic French kitchen. A well-made Hollandaise sauce, with the right balance of lemon juice and pepper over the salty richness of butter, deliciously complements the eggs, muffin, and surrounding potatoes.

The traditional technique for the sauce demands an annoying level of attention for a busy breakfast kitchen. It can also be a health concern if you don't have access to pasteurized yolks, because you have a small margin of error between reaching the necessary 135 degrees to kill the occasional salmonella and turning your sauce into scrambled eggs. Hollandaise is also difficult to store during service, demanding creativity to find the perfect spot around the stove that will have just the right temperature. If it gets too hot, it will break. If it cools too much, it will either need to be reheated and possibly break or, being too cold, it will fall from the top of your hot egg when you put it under the heat lamp, waiting for pickup.

Many restaurants take shortcuts, using other ingredients like industrialized mayonnaise, heavy cream, xanthan gum, cornstarch, or flour of all sorts to stabilize the Hollandaise. Some use Hollandaise sauce mix packets, to which you only add water. All that stuff is revolting. The beauty of this mother sauce is its simplicity: two yolks for about eight ounces of butter, one tablespoon of lemon juice or other acid, such as vinegar or reduced white wine, a pinch of salt, another of cayenne pepper, and a bit of water to adjust the consistency. Any other special items to make the preparation easy or the sauce stable will very likely corrupt the taste, and you might as well just call it something else. Anybody who takes their eggs Benedict seriously can tell the difference when the sauce has been adulterated, and I've yet to find a Hollandaise that tastes better with the added stabilizers.

This distinction between the authentic and the improvised goes for any other widely known sauces and dressings: balsamic vinaigrette, marinara, Caesar, ranch, and so on. You have a bit of flexibility on seasoning and garnishing, but when you choose to not use dill in your ranch dressing because you don't like the taste of the herb, you have to call it Chef Joe's Modern Ranch, to make the point that you've modified the recipe. It may well be that you have developed a better recipe. My vegan Caesar dressing is pretty tasty, but I ought to come up with a distinguishing name for it, so people realize that it has no Parmesan, yolks, or anchovies.

You must do this both out of respect for the tradition of the dishes and those who invented them, and to avoid disappointing clients like me, who expect that you use true buffalo mozzarella when it's quoted on the menu, because it feels and tastes different from regular fresh mozzarella; hence the appeal of the name.

Years ago, an American friend returned a Caesar salad at a restaurant in Rio de Janeiro because it contained no Caesar dressing and included ingredients that you wouldn't normally expect to find, like fresh green bell peppers, cucumber, and crumbled cheese. It was a regular salad with some type of vinaigrette. Caesar salad was an uncommon menu item in Brazilian restaurants those days. The waiter and manager, perplexed with the complaint, had no clue what a Caesar was supposed to be, and neither did the chef, but someone must have found the name catchy and decided to so baptize their salad.

If you want to use a famous dish name, you ought to do some research. Maybe you won't make the best jambalaya in your restaurant in Utah, but you should do some investigation and use the right ingredients. Otherwise, you are either trying to fool me or making a fool of yourself.

Be true to what you promise on the menu; assume people will know the difference. If your fish is frozen, omit the word "fresh." If you serve a chicken liver pâté, don't call it "fois gras," call it "hühnerleberpastete" and get a kick from watching your servers trying to pronounce it correctly in the dining room.

I eventually gave up ordering eggs Benedict at most diners and chain breakfast restaurants. I've had too many fake Hollandaises and heard too many sanitation horror stories. I order the spinach, mushroom, and cheese omelet, and that's usually what they bring to my table.

# Presentation

Some exceptionally artistic and elaborate cooks plate food so stunning, I almost feel sorry to eat it. I envy people with the fine skills for carving vegetables or placing precise drops of secondary sauces. Other cooks are more technical, focused rather on the precise execution of the food's composition, seasoning, doneness, and so on. Some cooks also absolutely loathe the practice of sculpting food into fine art, as if a colorful arrangement of the elements in the plate was somehow an offense to their professional dignity.

I'm in-between. I'm no longer fascinated by a block of rice perfectly shaped with a metal ring or a terrine cooled in a diamond-shaped mold. But I understand that these things can serve the purpose of keeping foods orderly. Moreover, the importance of food presentation is inherent to the human species, for during our evolution we learned to discern whether foods are safe by its appearance and to stimulate our digestive system at the sight of food. My discomfort begins when the presentation makes it difficult for me to manage the food or when I can't identify flavors because there are too many layers on the plate.

For me, as a client, food presentation serves three major purposes: to create visual pleasure and excitement for the meal, to create harmony among the components of the plate, and to give me a hint of where to start and how to combine the flavors in the plate. Plating has traditional rules: proteins are considered the main ingredients and are presented in the center of the plate, between a vegetable and a starch. Sometimes, one of the elements in the plate physically lifts another, to enhance the tridimensional perception of height and volume. Sometimes cooks coat their food with abundant sauce; other times, the chef may serve the sauce directly onto the plate and underneath the food, particularly when skillful knife cuts and grilling techniques make the slice of roasted eggplant a cross-marked beauty to behold.

You may want to keep in mind, though, that if I could have commissioned a portrait of my cat to Picasso, I would like to recognize my cat in the painting. If, unexpectedly, your Picasso chef goes cubistic on me, it will be an unpleasant surprise. I may not know where to find the components on the plate. Also, if your kitchen artist piles food like a game of Jenga, my dining experience may be more stressful then I had anticipated, and I'll close my evening with the unexpected task of scrubbing my shirt with OxiClean.

I personally prefer to eat the food components in the plate separately. For no particular reason, just habit, I often eat the roasted vegetables, then the kale, then the mashed potatoes, instead of combining bits of them all on the fork. When I do mix foods in my fork, like rice and beans, I like to have control over the proportions of each element I want in every forkful. If you serve the ratatouille atop the couscous, I'm left with no option but to eat them combined. Consider if laying foods on top of each other on my plate is absolutely necessary for your concept.

Also, what goes in the plate must serve a purpose. If you served a perfectly seasoned grilled tofu, don't add drops of herb-infused oils just because you believe the plate needs a little green coloring. Don't dust foods with dried herbs or Paprika, because dried herbs taste horrendous and paprika is only good once it's rehydrated and cooked.

A grilled Portobello cap is delicious with minimum seasoning from the marinade. You may want to serve it on top of a wine reduction, but there is no need to contrast the flavor with a raspberry and brie sauce, which may also be fantastic, but I'll probably eat separately, using the service bread. When the legendary Ferdinand Metz says that in cooking, less is more, it's wise to listen.

Finally, unless you are serving a happy meal, don't put anything on my plate that is inedible. That means that, for my safety, the olives should be pitted and that any device used to shape, truss, hold, or mold foods should be removed. Under no circumstances should you put a plastic flower, leaf, or any other synthetic form of garnish on my plate. I quit eating Play-Doh when I was seven.

# PART 2: HINTS FOR THOSE WHO MANAGE PEOPLE

## Motivation

As a good corporate citizen, every so often I would spend a portion of my Saturday in the office, catching up with the workload, cleaning up my e-mail, and getting ready for the following week. For years I had a personal policy of not bringing work home or opening my work e-mail when not at the office. I'm not productive at home, where I'm incapable of focusing. I easily succumb to the temptations of the many distractions available: food, DVDs, friends, wife, pets, etc., resulting in prolonged inefficient effort and less joy in my leisure. I'd rather go to the office, get things done, and get out.

One Saturday, I found at the office the unlikely presence of a good friend from human resources. He had a deadline for completing compiling the data of the employee satisfaction survey. Curious as a cat, I offered to help with categorizing the written comments of the survey and so I read through a few hundred remarks of my fellow employees.

For those of you who ever wondered, these surveys are truly kept anonymous, and your boss would probably not receive your specific comments, but a summary of the issues, categorized by clusters. That company had, at the time, forty thousand employees. I must warn you that it will be easier to find out who wrote what in a restaurant that employs ten people.

At the time, I was going through my MBA and had spent many class hours rolling my eyes during lectures on managing diversity, creating a friendly work environment, fomenting good work ethics, and developing methods of nonmonetary motivation for the workforce. All sounded cute, I thought, but I really worked for the money. More money was more motivation, simple as that. Save the money from the corporate picnic; give me a raise, and all is good.

When responding to the employee survey, I believed I had a moral obligation to my colleagues to respond "strongly disagree" to the question

"Do you believe your salary is equitable to the compensation paid for the same role in other companies?" Are they crazy? Who would ever respond, "Don't worry, my salary is fine," even if they believed it was? Human resources departments are well aware of people like me, so they don't really pay much attention to that question. They just put it there because a satisfaction survey would look silly without addressing compensation.

Well, what I learned that day was truly surprising and revealing. Most people were relatively satisfied with their salaries, ranging between "somewhat agree" to "slightly disagree." On the recurrence of written comments, dissatisfaction with compensation came in fourth place, third was "I don't understand the company's strategies for the future," second was "management is clueless," and first was "I would like more recognition for my good work."

An overwhelming number of people desperately wanted a pat on the back to go home walking on clouds. People greatly care for being acknowledged. That survey was proving once again that humans seek reassurance, hoping for occasional words of appreciation and praise for their efforts.

I am very self-critical and never expected much recognition from my managers. Some were better than others in that regard, but I knew when I had done a good job, so I saved them the trouble by reaching across my shoulder and patting myself. I must confess, though, that I was happier in the jobs where I found a good work environment, had fun with my colleagues, and made good friends. And, yes, getting occasional good feedback also reassured me that I wasn't just wasting my life down the drain, day in and day out.

If you are in the restaurant industry and expect to be cheered for your good work, you'll be waiting for a while. Traditional chefs, managers, and maitre d's often lack such soft skills. In fact, you are expected to toughen up and handle pressure, abuse, and yelling, keeping your mouth shut. Once a year, you might receive a Christmas bonus and hear "Thank you, keep up the good work." Bring a recorder to the kitchen that day, so you can replay those words when in need of positive reinforcement.

It really shouldn't be this way; why can't managers communicate better with employees? Yelling and intimidation shouldn't be the preferred forms of displaying leadership. A good performer should get a few appreciative words. If you make mistakes, your manager should try to help you. If you are hopelessly careless and incompetent, you should be fired, for restaurants can't afford to carry dead weight, but the temperamental outbursts are unnecessary. I've seen waitresses brought to tears and cooks storm out the door over escalation of the most trivial issues. Frankly, we spend more time at work than anywhere else. My colleagues see me for far more time than my wife does, and we shouldn't have to put up with so much silliness at work.

I've also seen good examples and heard promising ideas for creating a pleasant work environment, which results in a happier place to work, less absenteeism, reduced turnover, and better productivity. A good reading reference for restaurant managers is the book *Fish!* by Stephen C. Lundin, PhD, Harry Paul, and John Christensen. It discusses motivation and teamwork in reference to employees of Seattle's Pike Place Market, where they made lemonade out of a tough work environment. By playing with the clients and throwing fish across the stand, they made a rough job look fun and enjoyable.

I've compiled some good practices, which I've seen yield results in motivating employees.

- Let there be music in the kitchen. Music is OK during prep time, but not necessarily during service hours, when you need your attention undivided. Let them sing, dance, and shake their booties to relieve the stress. All within reason—your focus, of course, should be on the food.

- Create a kick-ass contest. Every now and then, the best performer in the kitchen goes home earlier and skips the end-of-shift cleanup. It doesn't always need to be your best cook, but could be the griller who made perfect marks, the prep cook who trimmed precisely and minimized waste, or the rookie at the salad station who held on bravely through a busy shift.

- Allow time for storytelling. Let the staff discuss anecdotes from the old days and recent cooking or serving experiences. There's always something to be learned and shared.

- Have an after-shift party from time to time.

- Do your utmost to communicate your criticism in a civilized manner and offer compliments when appropriate. A classical book called *The One Minute Manager* establishes a valuable rule: reprimands and compliments should be brief, preferably within a minute, and they should be specific and address the issue, not the person. You should say, "We need you to be more focused and work faster" instead of, "You are useless and lazy." Praise may be given in public, but reprimanding should be done in private, unless you are in a situation such as having to fire someone for theft, where you may choose to be discreet, while intentionally being less than 100 percent secretive, so that other workers can learn that you have no tolerance for such behavior. Most importantly, you must be fair and hold all employees to the same ethical standards, while the skill standards will vary by position, seniority, and pay level.

- Don't be too cheap. Give your staff a beer after the shift or let them take food home from time to time. This will improve camaraderie, reduce theft, and allow for better communication between you and your employees. It will also allow you to better choose and control what the staff is taking home. Some owners dislike the practice of employees taking home leftover food because they believe the cooks will inflate the amount prepared for the shift, but you must trust that the sous chef will be controlling the prep work. If you don't have someone you trust in control of the kitchen, you are in deep water anyway.

- Be fair with the work distribution when it comes to cleaning, receiving products, or attending the obnoxious clients. Don't let some people always get the easy tasks and others always get screwed.

- Don't abuse the dishwasher. I got furious when cooks and servers gave me hotel pans without first dumping the food content in the trash or scorched soup pans without filling them with soaking water. Don't ever drop cooking knives at the dishwasher station and warn about screaming hot sizzlers. An injured dishwasher will destroy a service shift. If he got a fourth-degree burn from a frying pan you dropped there, hidden within a bunch of sheet trays, you should be sent to his station while he goes to the hospital. Bring the dishwasher some food and invite him out for a beer with the big boys. Pay the good ones well, who work fast, don't break too many dishes, don't throw away silverware, and don't mind the job. They are hard to find.

- Don't be afraid to praise people, under the premise it will inflate their egos and they'll flee for more money. You can only have so many sous chefs, managers, and maitre d's; some of your excellent servers and cooks will, inevitably, leave for higher positions, and I can assure you that keeping their self-esteem low will not prevent them from going. If the server truly enjoys the work environment at your restaurant, she may not leave for another dollar per hour in a place she'd feel miserable. Or she may return and beg for her old job back.

- Create specific awards for extraordinary deeds: the senior waiter and a cook who did a great job receiving the health inspector when the owner, chef, and manager were nowhere to be found, the hostess who defused a major crisis with a party of fifteen who were somehow dissatisfied and wanted to leave, the cook who invented recipes that were more cost-efficient, reduced waste of products, or were just darn delicious. A good cook told me he'd be paid an extra hundred dollars every now and then for creating good specials that would fly out of the kitchen, while also managing the ripening and slow-moving items in the walk-in fridge.

Remember that you, as a manager or owner, wish to promote a culture of exceptional customer service, founded on true caring for the clients' happiness. How do you expect your employees to live and breathe this culture if you treat them like crap? Or how could you expect synergy if you are a chef who despises the crew in the front of the house?

Danny Meyer, owner of several successful restaurants in New York like Union Square Café and Gramercy Tavern, all highly praised for excellent customer service, stated that in his restaurants, the employees come first, and the clients second. He believes it impossible to promote great service without first taking care of the staff. These strong words could be easily misunderstood. He does not mean that the client isn't king in his restaurants. He means that a great work environment, surrounded with courtesy and respect, is a prerequisite for great service.

# Magic

My cousin is a magician, as in someone who performs in theaters, cutting people in half and making things disappear. He is one of those fortunate people who, since early childhood, knew exactly what he wanted to be. It took me almost 40 years to discover my dream. He got his first magic set when he was seven and never stopped training, developing spectacular manual skills and a bewildering understanding of how visual perception works. He builds his own equipment and, of course, everything is completely secretive. His tricks are truly puzzling; we know it's all based on deception and distraction, along with motor coordination and good engineering, but how the hell does he do that?

While my cousin does magic, your kitchen does alchemy. As renaissance mystics believed fire to be the crucial element in their pursuit of transmuting lead into gold, so does your kitchen transform ingredients into divine food, through the purification of flames. How do you do it? You may choose to reveal it to us, using an open kitchen concept, or conceal it, choosing the traditional kitchen style, of which we get just a brief glance when the busboy swings the doors. My feelings are mixed. While I personally love to watch the frenetic dance of a busy kitchen, I also believe the tricks are less exciting when we know how they're done. Also, the white walls and aluminum equipment under fluorescent lights are far less attractive than the décor in the dining room, so you may need to ask your architect and designer to rethink the kitchen, if you are going to make it part of our experience.

Even if you keep your kitchen veiled, we now live in a world where chefs have been raised from the status of blue-collar workers to celebrities. A lot of us would like to know who's cooking our food. Even if many chefs don't actually cook much, but just oversee the kitchen and expedite things, we still want to see them.

This provides a huge opportunity for you to elevate the clients' perception of your restaurant without spending any cash. If your food is halfway decent, you may want show your chef around; encourage him to bring the plates to a random table at the dining hall. The chosen clients will be impressed, and the other tables will be a bit envious, but pleased to see the wizard who makes the food magic. At a restaurant I worked, the chef and cooks often brought plates to the tables. Among other things, it made us take more pride in our plates and be even more careful with the cooking and plate presentation.

Let the chef walk around for a while, greet the diners, and ask questions about the food; specific questions for feedback that doesn't often reach the kitchen. "Do you like the matching of the seitan served with white beans and spinach? Is the Creole seasoning too spicy for you? Did you like the choices of soup?" Look at the plates and see how people are eating, how they combine food on their forks. Are they pushing foods to the side? Is the amount of sauce appropriate? Is your plating effective, or does the food collapse as they try to cut a piece? Are the servers placing the plates with the proper side facing the client?

Don't, however, allow the chef to spend too much time in the dining hall, even if he can afford to spare it. Make the chef's visiting time special. Also make sure the chef is presentable, wearing clean whites, good shoes, and no apron or side towels.

If the chef is not presentable to the public, perhaps lacking minimal social skills or looking like a mechanic after the oil-changing shift, the restaurant owner could do the social show. The owner holds far less culinary glamour than the chef, but her showing up and roaming around the tables will also impart the message that you care enough about the clients to take the time to socialize with them. If the owner also works as the front-of-the-house manager or hostess, her presence becomes more mundane, and it won't be perceived as a special treat. In that case, you'll need to get the chef to shave, comb his hair, trim his nails, and learn to speak some sort of articulate language.

When the chef is among the customers, I can assure you that someone will ask for a recipe. Magicians don't reveal their tricks, but don't be naïve; these days you can find a recipe for anything online, so don't say "All our recipes are secret." Tell the old lady how you make your special borscht. By the time she gets home, she won't remember it anyway. If she does, she won't take the time to make the stock or cook fresh beets; it will never taste as good as yours. If it took you 20 years to find the perfect combination of herbs and spices for a seasoning, you may preserve its confidentiality by being vague on your description of condiments. If they praise your frites, you may have to divert the conversation. You don't want to reveal that you buy a commercial brand of blanched and seasoned potatoes, ready for the second fry.

I once asked a chef why my soup tasted too starchy when I tried to thicken it with a flour-and-milk slurry. "You're not cooking it long enough," he said. "Flour takes twenty minutes to cook thoroughly. Also, use cornstarch for a slurry, or preferably make a roux or beurre manié. By dissolving the starch in fat instead of liquid, your food will taste better, and you will avoid lumps." I learned something, and my soup is much better these days. What I still can't figure out is how my cousin knew I had picked the queen of clubs.

# McD

I am the walking type of tourist. I like to feel the ground under my shoes, cross a busy road, look at people's clothes and faces, and touch the wall of a common building of no historic value. I like to get lost and see a side of town I would never have planned to visit, or at least that's what I tell my wife when we end up somewhere unexpected. I like to peep in people's homes and see what they are watching on TV. I like to see how locals go about their daily lives. My traveling plans must include very long walking days, from one side of town to another. Often this walking is necessary, due to limited parking near the important sites, and taxi costs quickly add up against my budget. Subways always provide a good option for moving quickly, but not so great a choice for sightseeing. I prefer walking until the last signs of fatigue send me back to the hotel: blisters on the ankle from the new shoes, pulsating pain in the soles of my feet, rash between the legs, back pain, and a very moody wife.

When walking in a strange city abroad, miles away from my hotel, every so often—in fact, very often—I will need a bathroom. Public restrooms are not as abundant abroad as they are in American cities, where you can find them in shopping malls and public parks. Abroad, you must find someplace to have a snack to get nature's commanded relief. In the first few days, I will try the local cafés and experience the charm of the European ambience. Some cafés are in buildings just as old as America itself and are well worth the visit. Locals hang out, loudly discussing politics and soccer, with occasional pauses to check out some *bella donna* passing by. A few people read newspapers from cover to cover over the same lonely cup of coffee.

By the third day, I realize that the strategy of visiting local cafés for my restroom needs has two major shortfalls. One, each cappuccino that I feel compelled to order to use the bathroom costs about seven bucks (which may be the answer to the question, "where did my money go? I swear I had one hundred Euros yesterday morning!"). Two, many of the bathrooms have not been cleaned since Napoleon took control of Rome and had the pope arrested, and the concentrated odor of urine is intoxicating. I can't personally report on the ladies' restrooms, but I'm told they are not much better, which is a mystery to me, for I fail to see how women would miss their target as some of us men do.

After much reluctance, I eventually give in and adopt McDonald's as my new best travel friend. You see, I make an honest effort to avoid eating in American chains when I'm abroad, but I must admit that McD, Burger King, Pizza Hut, Subway, and others conveniently provide less expensive meals and, very importantly, clean bathrooms.

I'm not sure if these companies realize how much I and many travelers appreciate the availability of their clean WC facilities in times of distress. I consider it to be one of the noblest acts of public service provided by the food industry. Companies spend a sizable portion of their budgets sponsoring charitable foundations, civic organizations, and children's sport activities as a form of building a good reputation in their communities and society overall, but we can't understate the importance of the available restrooms. At smaller restaurants, I am uncomfortable to rush in looking for the loo, while in these chains, it feels natural. Most often than not, I will consume something. If nothing else, I'll get an item that Europeans have yet to learn to appreciate: a large soda with a generous amount of ice.

To my dismay, I'm seeing an increasing number of fast food stores install locks on their bathroom doors or even charge a fee for the use of the restroom. Please! Stop! No matter what marketing funds you may need to cut, don't mess with the bathrooms. Please invest the money to keep them clean and put up with the eventual bums and crackheads. This will yield immense returns in building a good reputation with the public, demonstrating that we're always welcome.

Here in Pennsylvania, one evening as I drove back from my grad school, I had a serious intestinal situation. As I entered the highway portion of my commute, I felt an intense pain in my lower abdomen, excruciating cramps like I had never experienced, nor have I ever since. Something needed to leave my system immediately. The agonizing pain came in cycles. I would endure thirty seconds of contracting every muscle below my belly in effort to keep the exit tightly closed, followed by a moment of relaxation before the next wave came. I drove considerably fast in a section of the road often infested with ticket-happy police. As I evaluated my possibilities, the scenarios didn't look good. The road's shoulder was very narrow, and I didn't have minimum privacy or any means of potentially cleaning my mess. Letting things happen in the car would be a cleaning nightmare and rushing to get somewhere quickly could result in a very awkward interaction with law enforcement. I was still thirty minutes away from home, and I knew I didn't have that much time. Letting it go seemed an increasingly inevitable reality. I started to evaluate how to minimize the damage, how I would go about cleaning the car, and how I would walk from the parking lot to my townhouse in such state, given the frequent vigilant watch of my nosy neighbors.

The only thread of hope I had to cling to was a McDonald's five miles away, when the highway converts to a business road. Indeed, McD once again saved the day. I rushed into the store in complete despair, found the restroom open and unoccupied, and didn't have the time to shut the door of my stall. Before I could even sit, it was as festive as the Fourth of July. It was powerful, and it wasn't pretty. The sense of relief is still unmatched. I got a mountain of paper, hand soap and water, and cleaned my mess as well as I could. Then I pulled myself together, and although I wasn't hungry, I bought some French fries and a milkshake and drove home. I wouldn't have made it if the restroom door was locked and I'd had to find the manager for the keys. It was a close call, and I was immensely grateful to McDonald's.

Many businesses post signs restricting the use of the restrooms, in the same way that other businesses post signs of "No turnaround" in their parking lots to prevent some unadvised lost driver from using their pavement to make a safe U-turn. Well, I believe it is not in the best interest of a business to tell people to "Stay away from our property." It simply doesn't resound well, and as a rule, you should avoid it. So I'm in a street festival and desperately need to pee, or I made a mistake, got lost, and need to turn around. It happens to all of us. Is it nice to find a sign saying "Don't come here for help?" Of course not. I may forever lose my interest in your restaurant because you post unwelcoming messages.

When streets are closed for seasonal festivities and people are roaming around, it may be a good business day for you. Or maybe the folks will choose to snack with the street vendors, which could hurt your business. Many will need a restroom, and that might be the first opportunity for people to enter your restaurant and see what you are about. Who knows? It may entice people who hadn't ever noticed you to return for dinner the following weekend. It may promote your name and generate a few new clients. How much did it cost you?

Don't think of it as a burden, the cost and effort of keeping your restroom available and clean; think of it as a marketing investment.

# The Actor's Principle

Stage acting would have been my career of choice, at least when I went to college, had I been willing to brave the fear of starvation that comes with the profession. For every actor that reaches fame and fortune, hundreds struggle to make ends meet. But at the time, the acting classes, rehearsals, and stage time were pure fun: the informality, the strange people, the emotional trips that you make yours, and the possibility of becoming anyone or anything are bliss for people like me who love change and are easily bored. My talent was as far as anyone can be from being a Marlon Brando, so it was probably wise to give it up.

My major setback was that I took myself too seriously, an unfavorable trait for an actor. In that profession, you must divest yourself of any self-consciousness, pride, vanity, and shame so you're liberated to shape yourself into whichever character you might be assigned.

My first acting teacher gave us a few pearls of wisdom. One of them I remember vividly to this day. Observing the behavior of couple of extras on the stage, he stopped the rehearsal and gave us a speech. "This stage is forty feet wide, the audience is in the dark, and there are tens of kilowatts of light directed to the scene. The public is watching everything that happens under the lights, so whenever you are on the stage, you are not 'hanging,' you are acting. If you were assigned to be a tree on a corner of the stage, you are a tree with all the purpose of your soul. Be a tree: stand as a tree, breathe as a tree, and think as a tree. You must act from the inside out. You must believe you have roots, you must feel the wind blowing your leaves and the photosynthesis in your cells. If you don't believe it, neither will the public. There's a reason you're there, so don't take it lightly."

I've seen servers and hostesses just "hang." It's disconcerting; like an unconvincing tree, it ruins the whole scene. If you haven't had a chance to watch the opera *Carmen* by Bizet, I suggest you make an effort to overcome any prejudice you might have against operas and give it a shot; it's a wondrous spectacle. In one scene of the first act, the Spanish soldiers watch the cigarette factory workers, all women, come out from their shift. This scene is your first glance at Carmen. There are some thirty people in the scene. The soldiers are at ease and joking around, but they act with the leisurely composure that soldiers display when still wearing uniforms. The workers look tired, but glad to be done with the shift, as cooks and servers look when the cleaning is done, the door is closed, and they are ready to party. The cigarette factory workers are smoking! God knows what legal and insurance miracles were pulled off with the city of New York so the cigarette factory workers could have a lit cigarette on the stage in the Metropolitan. Why go through that trouble? Because smokeless cigarettes would discredit the characters and ruin the entire scene.

As a waitress, every time you are visible, you are in the scene, and you must perform according to certain expectations. Be present, be mindful, and be convincing. If you need a break, get out of the scene, or you'll ruin the atmosphere of the restaurant. Do not allow me to witness, as I have too many times, your texting abilities, your lengthy chat with a fellow server, or your snacking.

Also behave within the framework of your character: even if you follow your lines to the letter, I assume your screenplay probably doesn't call for you to shout, yell, or scream, so don't spoil your interpretation by interacting loudly with the busboy.

Immerse yourself in your character and become the tree, albeit a courteous, attentive, and agile one.

# Take It Outside

Once I saw a client complain about the order; it was not what he expected. The server explained that it was exactly as described on the menu. She didn't want to take it back and face the temperamental chef/owner. The manager arrived and started arguing with the server, and finally the chef arrived and yelled at both the server and the manager for mishandling the situation.

I am the kind of guy that likes watching. Conflict, I mean. Not the fabricated situations in reality shows, but a real and honest confrontation. I don't like the WWE wrestling. I like the Ultimate Fighting, but the original ones, classics, with no stopwatch or point counting. The fights would only end with a knockout, a tap on the floor, or the referee, Big John McCarthy, deciding it would be irresponsible to allow one of the fighters to linger in the octagon. Maybe I like watching tension between other people because I go out of my way to avoid confrontations. Watching couples argue or work colleagues get in each other's faces does bring some voyeuristic pleasure.

That night, I had some fun watching the blame game between the server and the manager and the rudeness of the chef/owner, who was probably the original cause of his employees mismanaging the situation. My wife freaked out. Noticeably uncomfortable, she wanted me to stop watching. She wanted the check.

Despite the unintentional entertainment factor, let's be honest: it is extremely unprofessional to have a scene on the floor. Under no circumstances should the staff argue in public. You must be clear-minded enough to tell your employee or manager that you want to finish your conversation out of public view. Since so many people still smoke in this industry, this would be a perfect time for a cigarette break. Try to the best of your capacity to chill for a few moments, rethink the whole situation, and measure your words carefully. Words will come out badly when you are hotheaded.

If you have an unreasonable dissatisfied client, the best thing to do is make sure he or she goes away as quickly as possible: speed up her order or apologize that you are unable to meet his demands. Foot the bill, cut your losses, and move on rapidly. Some people cannot be pleased, and some leave their homes in a perverse search for aggravation. You can only hope they won't come back, or you may even need to deny them future reservations after a couple of occurrences. An argument with the client is not worth the effort.

You must realize that the issue is not about principles and who is right or wrong, it's about preserving the integrity of your workplace for yourself, colleagues, and clients.

On another occasion, I was having lunch at a small and unpretentious vegetarian buffet at the back of a health food store when a commotion arose: a disproportionately outraged client couldn't find a clean fork, and he started arguing with the cooks. We then learned that no one was at the dishwashing station, and the dirty china and flatware were piling up while the cooks busily tried to catch up with refilling the buffet pans. The store manager eventually showed up and took responsibility, but not action. The client's food continued to cool off while his head heated up. The manager apologized in what, to the client, seemed to be a condescending tone, which made matters worse. The scene kept going on and on to the point that I was getting ready to tell the client to fuck off and the manager to wake up. The client wasn't particularly profane, but he was way too aggressive for a totally Zen store. From the very beginning, when a simple "Excuse me, would you please find me a clean fork?" would have sufficed, he chose to go down the "Why can't I find a damn fork? Why is the service here always so bad?" route.

Despite him being a jerk, the whole discussion was worthless and pointless. Everybody lost: client, cooks, manager, and all of us hoping for a tranquil lunch. Had somebody quickly fetched and rinsed a fork and offered a brief and sincere-sounding apology, we would have witnessed a short and uneventful exchange of words, rather than a major escalation of tempers. Resist the temptation of engaging in the argument, and just let it go. Don't let your ego lead you to a time-wasting debate that cannot be won.

A possible exception is if a client behaves excessively abusively and profanely to your staff, in which case I would hope someone with managerial responsibility would back the staff up and tell the client that such behavior is unacceptable and that she or he should leave the establishment at once, please. The other clients will support you. Your employees are entitled to their dignity, and if someone is offending them, you must intervene in their favor.

So here is the rule of thumb: you cannot take the client into the kitchen or the back alley to discuss your differences in private, so handle the client with an honest apology and a quick, reasonable fix to the issue. Take internal staff quarrels out of public sight to sort them out. And if you choose to get physical in that back alley, please let me know. I'd like to watch.

# Noise Management

Where I grew up, there are clear distinctions between clubs, bars, and restaurants. You go to restaurants for the food; bars, for the drinks and eventual food; and clubs, well, to pick up a date, usually after many drinks. More specifically to this chapter, each has noticeable distinctions on the level of noise and the ability to sustain a clear conversation. When I went to clubs, I wasn't always at the peak of my sobriety, and my communication wasn't necessarily articulate, so the loudness of the music helped mask the fact that I wasn't making any sense, while conveniently allowing me to get very close to the girl I was addressing, phrasing whatever nonsense came to my mind with my mouth about three-fourths of an inch from hers. I've learned from a master in courtship that the topic of the conversation is irrelevant; what matters is the connection.

Having long been out of the flirting game, the loudness of bars here in America has become an annoyance to me. Nowadays I expect to actually have a conversation with my friends over a few beers. I don't know what to tell you, bar owner, because I know that for a lot of people, the place is not bombing if it lacks the noise level of a jet plane taking off, but I suggest that you understand the demographics of your target market, and be aware that people like me, who might well be a minority, will consider low noise as an important factor in selecting a bar.

I usually find the bar sections of fine dining restaurants to be more agreeable to my comfort level of decibels, but this also seems to be changing. Last week I went to a fairly large and yet fancy café, priced for a more selective clientele and decorated elegantly. By 9:30 p.m., the music volume cranked up drastically. College basketball was on the big screens at the bar, and the night was totally happening. The bar and restaurant were separated only by a four-foot-tall wall. Our evening became uncomfortable from that point on. We simply could not converse anymore, so we rushed to get the check and leave.

While aesthetically, the place looked perfect for the more mature demographic, the noise was unreasonable. The restaurant tables were not occupied to more than 60 percent of capacity, with little rotation, which is not good at all for a Friday night. Clearly, the bar was a profitable business and made up for any restaurant deficit. After my experience, I have no doubts that I won't be returning for dinner, except maybe a few years from now, for the early bird special. The food was

OK, but the vegetarian options weren't the best the house had to offer, an eggplant Parmesan, a touch undercooked, and an unmarinated grilled tofu, but the loudness ultimately made that restaurant an impossibility for me.

All my friends have now engaged in the very rewarding (or so I'm told) venture of parenthood, and they will often bring their children with them when we go to restaurants. We are a loud group even without the children, lively talking about politics, religion, sex, and any other topics capable of offending the neighboring tables. The only upside to having the children along is that we tone down the language, but the addition of children increases the distance between the adults participating in the conversation, and we have to project our voices over eventual and inevitable crying. If you hold seven children, ages one through four, at a table for two hours, I guarantee one of them will cry—possibly they all will, but hopefully not all at the same time.

I personally don't mind their presence. These kids behave significantly better than average, all very sweet and convivial, and I like them very much and am happy to be around them. Sometimes, however, two of them will dispute a toy and suddenly decide to settle it with a full-lung vocal contest. It's white noise to me, but I feel sorry for the couple, celebrating their fortieth wedding anniversary in that restaurant, that was unfortunately seated beside our table.

Last month, three of us men were at a Chinese restaurant with five children, while the wives had their night out. The place was half full. It had a small room for large groups, which was occupied when we arrived, though not for too long, and another room with ten tables or so, which wasn't in use. We were seated at a table surrounded by couples and small parties. They connected three tables for us, blocking the passage for the service staff and the path for the other patrons to the restroom. The kids behaved well that night, but I can't say that we were always quiet.

Too often, there seems to be little planning on how to accommodate the different types of groups and their noise levels. You may want to segment your seating area, having separate segments for large and small groups, placing children, in any numbers, in the area of the large groups. Mind you, I don't want to only pick on children. Groups of young adults on their "singles' night" or large groups of those of us not so young anymore, in various combinations, can make quite a thunder.

If you have a bar, try to insulate it from the restaurant seating area. I know it makes it harder for me to keep track of the score of the Penn

State game, but it's a sensible thing to do.

During your construction phase, plan to offset the reverberation of sound waves produced by hard floors and walls. Beware, for example, of the ceramic flooring my brother installed in his entire house: that material is an acoustic miracle! In the living room, you can hear a whisper from the bedroom even with closed doors and the TV on. Imagine how much noise I would be able to hear at your restaurant if you have ceramic floors and no treatment for the sound. Use ceiling treatments to absorb sound waves. There are numerous products on the market, made of fiberglass, foam, plaster, or fabric, that claim to absorb up to 75 percent of the sound that would otherwise bounce back down to the dining area. Compared to the many other costs of building or redesigning your restaurant, the investment is relatively small.

I've a good friend who once was a bartender. She barely spoke English at the time, and the bar was so loud she couldn't hear a word of what the clients ordered, so she often chose randomly which drink or beer to serve. Thanks to youth and a good figure, as well as generous servings, her tips kept coming solidly despite the fact that people rarely received what they actually ordered. I personally prefer that you pour the actual beer I chose, so please give your bartender a chance to hear me.

# You Gotta Go When You Gotta Go

I suspect my bladder is not very large; one beer, ten minutes, and I have to go. While my wife will endure excruciating pain to avoid using a public restroom, I will probably get to know your WC.

As a cook, I happen to know that kitchens are thoroughly cleaned every day, if not at the end of every shift. It is unimaginable that you will close your doors at night without cleaning your equipment, tools, and floors, and without preparing for the next day. You simply wouldn't be able to operate or survive the sanitary inspection from your local health authority. So I usually assume that your kitchen is relatively clean. All rules have exceptions, and I have witnessed some appreciable levels of filth, but most restaurants with dirty kitchens will not stay in business long. If not because of poisoning their customers, because poor cleaning habits are symptomatic of all kinds of other bad behaviors that will eventually bring your business to ruins.

Most people don't know about the daily kitchen cleaning procedures, making it possible that they will judge your cleanliness by the dining hall—if the dining area is filthy, you probably won't be in business too long, either—and by your restroom. The judgment of your food and sanitation practices based on your bathroom can be utterly unfair. It could be that a messy client left the restroom just before I entered or that you haven't assigned responsibilities for cleaning the bathroom as clearly as all the other duties in your restaurant. I suggest that you give the bathroom's cleanliness its due importance and move it up in your priorities.

- Please clean it often and thoroughly; some clients lack basic civility and will leave messes behind them.

- Make sure it has hot water for washing hands, which is a sanitation requirement for your staff, if they use that bathroom.

- Refill the paper towel dispenser. If you have ecological or budgetary reasons to use an air dryer, please invest the money to buy one that blows enough hot air to actually dry hands, so I don't have to wipe my hands on my trousers. Last weekend, at the movies, I used a dryer of the Xlerator brand, which was very impressive. Dyson's very expensive dryers also work well.

I have the habit of washing my face when I wash my hands, and I'm forced to use toilet paper to dry my face when paper towels aren't offered. All my friends know of this habit of mine, because I display tiny bits of the delicate white toilet paper all over my face when I return to the table. I never have been able to dry my face with the air dryer.

- Build your restrooms with materials that are easy to clean and dry quickly. The easier it is to clean, the happier you'll make your employees assigned to the task and the quicker you can make it available to the clients.

- Have some minimal taste in decoration and lighting. Even at nice homes, people invest a lot of cash in painting, furniture, decorative objects, and lighting fixtures for the guest areas, but they often neglect the restroom, which is part of your guests' experience. At the houses I have lived in, I made sure the lavatory was repainted, the fixtures were updated, the vanity and mirror didn't look like leftover construction material, and the toilet bowl was of a size that would accommodate a life-size adult.

- Have extra toilet paper available for emergencies.

- Install privacy walls between urinals. In multiple episodes of *Curb Your Enthusiasm*, the brilliant Larry David brings good attention to the topic.

- Offer as much privacy in the stalls as your budget can afford. Mind the height of the stall walls—some of us are taller than four feet and five inches—and the gaps between the walls and doors, to avoid providing too much unnecessary information on the activities being performed inside. Taller stalls, with better sealing and doors that come closer to the floor, cost more simply because they require more material. In the historical ancient Greek city of Ephesus, now part of Turkey, there is a well-preserved set of latrines from an ancient public bathroom. It's a long and undivided row of marble stone with keyhole-shaped cuts for side-by-side peasant relief. My friend Kristen was constipated for weeks just from the trauma of the sight.

- Have baby-changing stations in both the male and female restrooms so the fathers can handle the task. Fathers take their children out, too.

- Have proper treatment for odor, but don't overpower the bathroom with pumpkin pie essence. Why would anybody want to associate the smell of food with a bathroom? When it comes to odor management, ice in the urinals works well, for it cools the liquid, reducing its vapors, while the slow melt provides a permanent flush.

# Feedback

The average response rate for comment cards in restaurants ranges between 2 percent and 10 percent, depending on how much incentive you give your clients to fill in the card. The results have questionable statistical validity due to the small response rate and the fact that a particular profile of people are more likely to respond to the questionnaire, creating an inherent bias to your data. But you should offer questionnaires anyway.

Even if you take the time to walk around the floor asking the same questions, many clients will not tell the truth to your face, making the cards a vital source of feedback. Use the questionnaire to get honest input on questions like "Is the seating comfortable? Did you find the food properly seasoned? Did you like the menu choices? Was the wait time reasonable?"

I've completed a few, and I am personally more diligent in responding when there is a $5 gift certificate involved or a drawing for $1,000.

I went to a brewery restaurant that my friends adore, but where I'm often reluctant to go because it's always crowded and the beer selection is confusing. All the beers have funky names, none of which are sufficiently revealing about the beer's characteristics. The food and beer were good; the service was not. The server disappeared for unreasonably long periods of time; we even had to ask the hostess to help us get the check, and then we brought the check folder with a credit card directly to another server at the POS station, because our server was nowhere to be found. He may have had good reasons to vanish, but you would expect that he'd ask someone to cover for him.

At the table there were some noticeable pink cards, prepaid for mailing. I am filling it in now. The card has fourteen questions, two of them with multiple items, plus a section for written comments. It took me three minutes and forty seconds to complete, without filling in the fields with my name, address, phone number, and e-mail, all of which I will leave blank. I can assure you that it is unreasonable. Sounds like just a few moments, but very few strangers will give you four or five minutes of their time. Try counting three hundred seconds out loud and see how long it feels. Some hospitality schools make you do that, to feel the customer perception of being unattended for five minutes. It was a poor execution of a good idea. They are on the right track asking for feedback, but they slid off the road by asking for too much. All questions were relevant, ranging from who I am in terms of age and interests and then inquiring on several aspects of food and service. There were just too many questions.

An alternative approach could be breaking the questions into multiple cards and rotating them. One week, ask about demographics; another time, ask about the food experience. If the server encourages me to respond to some three questions, I'm very likely to do it. I'm not sure about fourteen. Next time your marketing guru designs a survey card for you, tell her to pull up a chair and stare at you while you fill in the sample form.

# Drink Your Poison

What do cooks eat? Anything they can get their hands on during their shifts, including ingredients at the stations and all kinds of trimmings of stuff that was cooked, but didn't make it to the plates. Servers also eat all they can get a hold of, but having less access to food from the stations, they hit the bread warmer drawers really hard.

I knew a cook who was addicted to peanut butter and jelly sandwiches, so he kept his own jars in the stove's refrigerated base. Another cook made spectacular sandwiches from slow-moving items in the pizza station—he was smart enough not to go 86 on items he would need for service—and an observant chef could have built a fantastic lunch menu out of those sandwiches. If you are a chef or kitchen manager who allows staff to eat from the stations, explain the etiquette about expensive items, depleting the station before service rush, and unsanitary eating over the food preparation area. Also pay attention to what they eat, and you may find new inspiration for your menu.

I believe it's unrealistic to prohibit cooks from eating your food. So to manage employee hunger in an orderly fashion, many restaurants cook family meals for the staff, which is also a good opportunity for a quick staff meeting.

How often, though, does the staff have the opportunity to experience the same service and food that the clients at your restaurant do? You should make sure that your staff, kitchen and floor, actually eats at your restaurant every so often, as clients. Maybe twice a year, give them a voucher for a dinner for two. It will allow them an opportunity to enjoy your food and show it off to someone, but more importantly for the business, will give the staff an opportunity to observe the restaurant from a different perspective and to critique the service, food, and the overall dining experience.

This can be insightful for you and your employees. Ask them to fill a comment card at the end of the meal and make sure to spend a couple of minutes with them the next day discussing their impressions.

Do not, however, eat among the clients during your shift or in your uniform. I don't want to see you chewing while carrying a food tray, or holding my plate with greasy hands from the sandwich you're nibbling at the service station. I once entered a small and empty restaurant in the middle of the afternoon and found the owner/host/server at a table with a plate of food. I felt bad for interrupting his meal, and I was too embarrassed to leave. It was uncomfortable to watch him having a forkful of food on every trip, halfway between our table and the kitchen.

If your cooks refuse to eat at your restaurant, you can't have a clearer indication that you have a serious problem.

# In Sickness or in Health; for Richer or for Poorer

In the preface of this book, I mentioned a study that found that 59 percent of restaurants fail within three years of launch and that the frequently cited success factors for restaurants are location, food quality, differentiation, and service. However, when I invert the question and ask what makes restaurants fail instead of what makes them succeed, I get two additional factors, which maybe we should label as "failure factors."

One important factor in failure is poor financial planning, often through unrealistic estimates of sales and operating costs, resulting in actual profits insufficient to pay all the bills, the business loans, and the owner's home mortgage. Most businesses take a while to take off, and many owners run out of money during construction and can't survive the initial months when the restaurant runs in the red. As a rule, these deficit months are likely to last a while. There might be room for you to run your business more efficiently, rationalizing staff scheduling and reducing waste, and you may be able to maneuver your business back to break even until you reach the brighter days. But if you have maxed out your line of credit and depend on the restaurant's income to sustain your family, you are a candidate for a dangerous spiral of debt, because you will start to default on payments, and the resulting interest will start to hit you like the Mike Tyson of the old days. The solution for that is to begin with the right amount of capital, so that you have a cushion of funds that will come to the rescue of your cash flow. Many restaurants fail, not because they had a bad concept, food, service, or location, but because they ran out of fuel to complete the upward climb towards making a profit. If you can count on funds to get you through this period, make sure that your business is truly growing. If all you see is a consistent downwards trend, draw a line for when you will conclude that you tried the best you could, when you will cut your losses and move on. Not every business is salvageable.

The other critical factor in failure is a bad partnership. Statistically, two types of partnerships are highly susceptible to failure: the one with your life partner and the one with your business partner. Finding that business partner who has the same level of commitment that you do and who will contribute an amount of money or labor equal to what you are contributing is nearly impossible. It's also unlikely that an investor will give you the money and let you run your business without interference. Furthermore, expectations change with time, and what seemed like a fair agreement may later look like a mistake. If you found a person to contribute 90 percent of the money, while you put in the labor and expertise, you might eventually get frustrated that your partner shares the profits while you are the one breaking the sweat. Or, conversely, he who invested the capital may be frustrated that you aren't delivering results.

It can be difficult to manage the long-term relationship of a partnership when it comes to making important decisions, dividing responsibilities, or simply co-managing the day-to-day business operations. You could even find a partner that will take unethical advantage of the facts that she is managing the finances and that you are totally illiterate in matters of accounting.

In restaurants, to make matters more complicated, your business partner frequently is also your spouse. In fact, once you signed your house as a guarantee for the loan, you're riding together, no matter what your LLC's operating agreement says. On the upside, I would hope that this removes the challenges of going into business with someone you don't know very well. I presume that you can make a good judgment of your husband's skills, commitment, character, and ethics. The drawback of couples working together comes from the emotional attachment between them, and from the bias of their marital relationship's dynamics interfering with the cold business decisions that need to be made. When it comes to dealing with my wife, the statement that "It's business, not personal" will not fly. If I make a business decision that offends her or hurts her feelings, I'm back on the couch, and even if I'm right, I'm stuck with the label of being stubborn. The fact is few relationships are strong enough to survive a 24/7 exposure to each other, and many marriages grow bitter when they are in business together, especially when times are tough at the restaurant.

Don't get me wrong, many couples have done it with success and so can you, but it's a good start to have awareness of the challenges posed by the day-to-day coexistence at work. If your tempers start to conflict from the get-go, you may want to consider a very clear split of responsibilities and possibly to schedule yourselves to work on different shifts.

While searching for real estate, I came across a fully equipped restaurant that became available because the owners, a married couple, had divorced, and they had to liquidate the allegedly successful business to settle the separation. The broker, a man of an age that can claim to have seen much in life, told me he could spend all day telling stories of businesses that closed due to either a divorce or a partnership fight.

A partner can be a great thing for your business, but make sure you are as selective in choosing your business partner as you were in picking your spouse. Then manage the relationship with as much care as you manage your marriage, and work hard to stay happy ever after.

# PART 3: NOTES FOR MY FELLOW CLIENTS

## The Golden Rule

I couldn't say it better than Jon Stewart in providing a guideline for social conduct: "general rule: don't be a douche."

# Revolution

You must tip. Make no mistake about this. Except in cases of utter negligence, absolute incompetence, or rudeness, you have to tip within the range of 10 percent to 20 percent. Try to tip round figures, by rounding up. Servers are usually paid cash for the tips at the end of the shift, and this will make the process a bit easier.

I personally don't like the concept of gratuity, partly because it doesn't feel right to me—it brings me a connotation of condescension—and partly because I believe it's a misrepresentation of the menu price, when, after adding tip and tax, I'll pay $25 for a dish listed for $19.99. Commercial trades should have clear prices, and tipping is a distortion of this system. This is similar to a dealer advertising a car for $17,000 and then adding $700 for "destination charges," or a product announced online for $10, but that requires another $9.99 for standard shipping and handling.

I've come to be more comfortable with tipping workers of the hospitality industry, but I can't come to tip the independent plumber who is already charging an indecent sum just to show up at my house. Last year I tried to tip the digital cable guy who did a professional job wiring my entire house, but he absolutely would not accept it, so go figure.

Records of the practice of tipping in America date back to the colonial times, but after the Civil War, a handful of states started a movement to ban the practice of gratuities, because it was associated with a class system in which the aristocrats tipped their social inferiors. With time, as we know, the practice became the *modus operandi* of the hospitality industry in America, and an important portion of its workers' compensation. Waiters are paid as little as $3.25 per hour in fixed wages, and the tip is expected as a complement to their earnings.

The law establishes that no one may be paid less than the state minimum wage, which cannot be lower than the federal minimum wage, so restaurant owners set wages very low for servers, expecting that, once the gratuities are added, it will likely exceed the minimum wage.

The restaurant owner must calculate the difference every week or month, depending on the local law, between the sum of the wages and the gratuities, and what the minimum wage would have been for the same hours, and match the minimum wage amount. Very rarely is a match necessary, but when it is, meaning that servers are being paid minimum wage at best, you will see a dramatic drop in the quality of the server staff.

When you don't tip, you are lowering the server's income for that day, but probably not enough to force the restaurant to complete his wages, so you are hurting only the server, not the restaurant. You are not starting a revolution, changing the system, nor teaching anyone a lesson. It is not the server's fault that they need your tip to complete their salary to a market rate for the profession. They may even agree with you that the tip portion should be part of their fixed salary. Some goodhearted restaurant owners would like to be able to pay a higher fixed salary to their servers, but in this very competitive market, a significant increase on their payroll costs would make their good intentions very short-lived.

In most of Europe, servers indeed have a higher fixed wage, and significant tips are only expected from American tourists. I've been yelled at by Spanish friends when I threatened to leave a 20 percent tip in a restaurant in Madrid. "No, no, no! Just leave the coin change!", which was less than two Euros for a forty-Euro tab." In America, you must tip.

# Force of Attraction

Most likely, she isn't flirting with you. She's working. She's smiling because she wants to be nice, not because she wants to go home with you. Apply some judgment. How drunk are you? How attractive are you? How attractive is she? If you were her, would you be flirting with you? Are you really, really sure?

OK, so you are convinced that she is interested in you; how do you go about this? On the very top of the list of what you can't do, as a good waitress friend of mine says happens regularly, is to say, "If you don't give me your phone number, I won't leave you a tip." This is disgusting, abusive, and frankly well worth a sexual harassment suit, or at least a glass of water to your face. I'm not sure what gives some clients the idea that the server is a prostitute. Even if she's dressed a little sexier than a nun, it doesn't give you the right to be abusive. If you intend to make arrangements for a personal escort, you should seek such business in a different venue.

Now let's, for a moment, assume that the fingers of destiny chose this moment to bring you and the lovely waitress together in true love. You are convinced beyond any reasonable doubt that something's happening and you can't let the moment pass. Love works in mysterious ways, and who am I to say it can't happen to you in a restaurant? Couples meet at work, hospitals, or even funerals. It's possible. Helen, a dentist friend, married a client of hers, and I can think of fewer more award conditions for flirting than having a root canal. I'll take your word that when you saw her taking the order, you knew in your heart that she'd be the mother of your five children. Violins sounded in the background; a breeze of spring flowers perfumed the air. An exchange of glances spoke more than a million words. This is it, it's real, and it's the moment of a lifetime. She is on the same vibe; she can't dissimulate that she's melting for you.

Here's my suggestion, so you don't blow your chance to connect with the love of your life: please, take a deep breath and hold off. Your first approach to someone you are interested in is more likely to be successful if done in private. Finish the meal, pay the bill, and tip. Be generous, but not ridiculous. Let your friends leave the restaurant, then pretend you are coming back for something you forgot. Find her, and being as discreet as possible—she can get in trouble for flirting with clients—say, "I'm sorry if this is inappropriate, but I happen to have two tickets for the U2 concert next Friday, and my brother won't be able to come. Would you care to join me?" At the first sign of resistance, back off and wish her a great evening. You want to show virility and decisiveness, but you should also be gracious and allow your proposal to be declined. The harder and more persistently you push, the harsher the rejection you may get. Don't embarrass her in her own workplace.

If she happens to say yes, good luck finding a last-minute pair of tickets for the U2 concert.

# Kick the Dog

So you've had a rough day. Your wife filed for divorce, your boss yelled at you, and you need to spend $1,500 to replace the clutch system in your European car. You're angry at life and everything that crosses your way.

That night, you go out to eat at a busy restaurant, and the server runs a little behind. In your heart, you know that you're just waiting for an opportunity to vent all the pent-up frustration.

Lock yourself in quarantine until you can cool off. It happens to me, too. After spending too much time in an electronics store and waiting in line for the cashier, the security person by the door asks to see my receipt. He literally stands four feet from the cashier and just saw the transaction processed and the receipt handed out. So why does he bug me for the receipt? I don't like to be interrupted, and my blood heats up. I overreact. I check the name tag on the cashier, Serena, and ask the security guy, Steve, if he has any personal problems with Serena. He doesn't trust her? She just processed the receipt and now he has to check it? Why should an internal control issue involve me? Either trust Serena or arrange another process with the store manager, but don't bring me into this. I make a little scene. On my way back home, I rethink the whole situation and regret having offended people, even if only with sarcasm. The employees were just following orders, whether they make sense or not. I need more self-control.

I vow to manage my reactions better, until I go to the supermarket and use the self-checkout machine. They have motion sensors that decide that I didn't use the right movement to place the item in the bag and the machine gets stuck. Impatiently, instead of waiting for assistance, I collect all items and move to the next machine and repeat the process, until all four of them are not operating. By that time, my wife has left and waits for me in the car, wondering why she married me.

I invariably regret such reactions, and I'm working on being a more patient and tolerant person. I'm getting better, one day at a time.

I bid you to try to do the same. Have some compassion. Look at the whole picture. Is the waiter trying his best? Is he being kind, polite, and apologetic? Keep in mind that his job is tough, too, and it's not his fault that the floor is understaffed. Don't take it out on him. Go home and kick the crap out of your stuffed dog.

# Don't Be Like My Dad

My dad is one of those guys that everybody likes. He is genuinely nice to all people and able to build rapport with anybody, from the doorman to the CEO. He's one of those people who become the painter's best friend while he's bargaining the price down by a third. His negotiation skills are truly admirable and a beauty to behold. Instead of trying to take advantage of a situation, he honestly looks for a win/win compromise. And he does it graciously and respectfully.

He's also a high-maintenance person who loves to get people involved in his common daily tasks. Once I took him and mom to visit Washington, D.C., where we spent a few days sightseeing the White House, the museums around the mall, Capitol Hill, the Lincoln Memorial, and the many charming streets of our capital. They had a great time. Unlike me, my dad loves to ask for directions and make all kinds of inquiries to random people, in Spanish, somehow assuming that everybody will understand him. At the Air and Space Museum while I was reading the visitors' guide, he managed to find much more information about the special demonstrations than I ever could: what they were, when they were, how interesting and what quality they were, and which one he'd like best. Finally, he got us escorted to some special seating at the IMAX Theater, for being a senior.

Back at the hotel, he decided he had eaten too much in our late lunch and just wanted some latte and toast for an evening snack. It was a decent hotel, but they didn't have room service. I explained that the hotel didn't have a restaurant, and the options in that area of DC on a Sunday night were limited. I went back to my room and ordered pizzas. By the time I got to his room with the food, he had already managed to speak to the reception desk, suggesting that someone, maybe the night guard, would have a thermos with coffee, and there should be some crackers somewhere around the hotel. A few phone calls later, apparently they'd found latte and crackers. Note that my dad doesn't speak a single word of English. "But Dad, I told you I was bringing pizza! Why would you want to drink the reheated coffee the night guard will need for staying awake all night?" To my despair, he called the reception desk, thanked them, and told them it was no longer necessary. (I begged him to accept the coffee after the staff had gone through all the trouble of finding it.)

When it comes to going with him to restaurants, I'm as embarrassed as a teenager being dropped off at school by his dad, dressed in pajamas. He is incapable of ordering a regular menu item. Ever. He grew up with particular food habits: nothing green but peas, no eggs except for omelets, no mushrooms unless minced, no onions, no pickles, no olives, no shrimp, and so on.

He will look at the menu as a guideline and assume all dishes can be served in any permutation of main item and sides, and that cooking methods can also be changed. He will request that the fish be baked instead of sautéed, that it comes with corn on the cob instead of fries, and that the broccoli can be replaced by anything that doesn't look threateningly green and healthy. By the time the server takes the entire order for the table and is making sure she memorized all the substitutions and requests, he'll ask something crazy like, "Do you have fresh passion fruit juice?" or explain that in Argentina, where he was born, the beef is more tender because they get the meat from younger animals. Please, Dad, the waitress doesn't care. You just made her lose her train of thought, which you didn't make easy with your order.

In his generation, everything was entirely customizable and made to order. He makes his requests with a natural sincerity and passion that leads people to pay attention. But he's also from a time of fully staffed restaurants and maitre d's fully knowledgeable in foods and beverages, who would build long-term relationships with the clients, learn their preferences, and make valuable recommendations. Nowadays people want their orders served in less than five minutes, and restaurants are often understaffed. Restaurants lack the time and resources for the level of customization my dad requires.

Dad, please, I implore you, make your order as simple as possible, and you'll minimize the chances that they will mess it up. But my plea is in vain. Mom is used to it. Judging from the look on her face, it doesn't bother her anymore. It drives me crazy. Amazingly, his order, more often than not, comes up right. His requests are so bizarre the waiter will actually memorize, make the correct notes, or come back to confirm: so instead of the coleslaw, you'll have mashed potatoes, without gravy, but with a warmed bleu cheese dressing, and you will have a soup bowl instead of the soup cup and the salad that regularly come with the entrée, is that correct?

From the cooking line perspective, when you are working on eight tickets at the same time, it's hard to pay attention to all the modifications to the dishes, and it disrupts the natural flow of the line. Even when the printer shows the substitutions in red ink, it undoubtedly increases the chances of cooks making mistakes.

Please, to the maximum extent permitted by your food allergies and palate aversions, try to keep your order simple, and things will go more smoothly for you.

# Dress Code

Rio de Janeiro is one of few cities in Latin America where it's socially acceptable to wear shorts for dinner in a finer restaurant. It's a shore city, and it's not unusual to see men and women in Speedos and bikinis walking through the streets, headed to or returning from the beach, among business people in suits commuting to work. My Colombian wife hasn't yet gotten comfortable with the sight. "Why can't they put some shorts on to walk to the beach?" she asks. Unattended things disappear quickly there, and you don't want to leave anything behind on the sand when you go for a swim. We dress and pack light when we go to the beach, or pack nothing at all. I personally have the self-consciousness not to wear Speedos, for I noticed it causes much discomfort to other locals, most of them quite fit and tanned.

Here in America, casual dressing is fair game. I love it. I spent too many years of my life working in suits, and I don't feel like wearing one in my leisure time.

Many corporations have now established policies of casual dressing, but they struggle to set good boundaries as to how far casual can go. I was convinced that one woman at the office wore her pajamas to work, with matching flip-flops. I don't mean to be the dress code police, but I believe you should abide by some minimal standards. Willing or not, when you dine out, you become part of the ambience as soon as you enter the restaurant. Assuming that a lot of effort was put into creating a pleasant environment for the patrons, you should be mindful not to ruin it for the other clients by wearing some outrageous outfit. If the restaurant you go to looks awful, well, you can still have some courtesy.

You don't need to wear a jacket and tie. In fact, I am not in favor of the few restaurants that still require such outfits, but when you are going to a relatively quiet and civil fine dining restaurant, you should refrain from wearing anything you wouldn't wear to visit your mom for Sunday lunch.

Women, consider how much of your breasts you really need to expose. No matter how much I may enjoy seeing them, it may cause discomfort among other people and could create marital issues for you and for others. A prolonged stare or even a quick glance at your twins could cause people to spend an uncomfortable night sleeping in the sofa. If your shirt exposes your belly, be critical as to whether your belly is really worth seeing. If you like tight pants, make sure they fit well, and no one will lose an eye if the whole thing explodes and a button flies off. My wardrobe consultant tells me that tight clothes don't make me look any thinner or manlier—much to the contrary, so I extend the warning to you. Leggings and Lycra tops won't suit your body type if you've relaxed a bit on diet and exercising. As to microskirts: c'mon, do you really want to look like you've been working the streets? Wear something over it, and take it off when you get to the club, where it's appropriate.

Men, although sleeveless shirts have unfortunately not yet been made illegal in all fifty states, they don't belong anywhere other than a gym, the beach, or a basketball court. No matter how big your biceps are, please never, ever wear them again in public, except for the afore-mentioned places. Armpits are arguably the least attractive parts of the human body, and I really would be happier if not exposed to the turf of hair in your axilla while I'm eating.

Guys and girls, I am from a generation that doesn't understand sag-ging, the practice of pulling down your pants to expose your underwear. Although I have to acknowledge the public service you are providing by cleaning the streets as you walk, I'm not sure what else it does for you. How is it a sign of toughness, to pull your pants to expose your ass? Where I come from, people would look at you a bit funny. And how can it be practical and comfortable to walk with your pants down to your knees? I do that at home, sporadically, when I run out of toilet paper and need to go fetch a replacement roll, and it feels very awkward. Your mom would probably yell at you if you showed up like that at her house, so we are back to the "Mom's house" guideline a few paragraphs above.

Filthy clothes don't pass the mom rule either.

Faces with more than ten piercings… Well, what can I say?

Every rule has an exception. In this case, it's that top models can wear pretty much anything.

# DUI

When I was younger, I had my occasions of excessive drinking at parties. I never did anything crazy during those days, nor did my conduct change much when I was high on alcohol. But I would wake up with that feeling that an alien ate my brains with a spoon while I slept, and I would vow never to drink that much again. Nowadays I have much better control over alcohol consumption, and I haven't had a hangover for as long as I can remember. I have a glass of wine or a bottle of beer on most evenings, and I'm blessed for not having a propensity for addiction.

Alcohol has been repeatedly proven to be healthy for your circulatory system, most especially red wine, because of the flavonoids and antioxidants abundant in darker grape skins. It may help increase your HDL ("good") cholesterol and help prevent inflammation in arteries and avoid blood clots. Too much alcohol can still help your arteries, but such benefits are offset by the damage done to your liver and kidneys, as well as the increase in blood pressure.

What you choose to eat and drink is a personal matter. Be aware of the health implications of your excesses and decide as you may. The issue I want to address is the impact of drunkenness on your behavior. I firmly believe that drinking doesn't turn anybody into an entirely different person; rather, it enhances personality traits that you inhibit while sober. As per the famous inscription at the Greek temple of Apollo at Delphi: "Know Thyself." Know your limits and what you are capable of doing when drunk, and spare us. Another inscription at the temple of Apollo read, "Nothing in Excess."

I have met many people over the years who act strangely after a few too many drinks. Some people get overly aggressive, verbally or physically; others become melancholic. I have a friend, Gary, who becomes a bit over-affectionate and compulsively hugs everyone around him at the bar. Another friend, Fred, just starts to laugh a lot, and my jokes suddenly turn out to be very funny.

Many of us, in different degrees, surpass our inhibitions and find it more spontaneous, for example, to flirt and address girls or guys in bars and clubs after having had a few. I have to admit that effect of booze has served me on occasions, and it has also made girls look significantly more interesting and attractive than they would have otherwise appeared to be.

I have no intention of judging you for drinking too much or for your behavior when you do so. But please find the appropriate venue to drink to excess.

Dining Under the Influence of alcohol (DUI) is an issue for restaurants. These establishments—different from bars, where bouncers are a necessary business practice—do not expect nor prepare for dealing with scandalous performances and annoying behavior from patrons. Neither are the other clients.

Alcohol has fantastic profit margins, helping balance less profitable menu items and paying for the high labor costs that every restaurant has to deal with. Many people enjoy a drink before or after their meals, or a bottle of wine that well matches their food, and some clients expect restaurants to offer alcoholic drinks, or they will go somewhere else. Thus, restaurants invest a small fortune in extortive liquor licensing and insurance premiums and undergo constant scrutiny of state officials in order to be able to offer alcoholic beverages. I met a man who, facing extraordinary and unexpected costs to repair sewage problems at his restaurant, fell behind on his liquor insurance premium. An inspector paid him an inopportune visit, and he was shut down, just like that. It was only one month before the Christmas party season, when the many booked celebrations would have pulled him out of the hole.

Be sensible on matching the style of establishment and how much you intend to drink. If you want to indulge or build courage to pick someone up, go to a bar or club. If you are known to become impertinent or abusive, drink at home, preferably by yourself or with someone bigger than you, who can take control.

Above all, of course, don't drive. I witnessed a man drive out of the parking lot of a bar, late at night, immediately cross to the wrong side of the road (on which I was driving) and hit a post, less than a hundred yards away from the bar. It was bizarre, one of those things you think you'd only see in movies. Like many, he probably thought he was still capable. A DUI can also be very expensive. A kid at culinary school had spent more than ten thousand dollars in related fines and legal fees. It's a very bad investment for your money.

A guy from my high school was a driver involved in a reckless accident where two people died. Another friend argued with me that that driver was a "good guy." Sorry, but he was racing, intoxicated, against another car on a major street and crossed two red lights before they finally lost control of the cars. Even at two in the morning, this was absurdly irresponsible. He deserved to spend a long time in jail; he killed people. Expensive lawyers got him out on parole way too soon. I have no idea what goes through the minds of individuals who have killed innocent people, nor how these folks can live with their consciences ever after. I can only guess how unbearable the remorse must be. Be sensible.

# Complaints

One evening, I added artichokes to a pizza that doesn't normally have artichokes. I reached for the six-pan of artichokes instead of the wild mushroom. A woman sent back the pizza, informing us of her allergy to artichokes.

Artichoke isn't among the most common allergens, but there are people who are allergic to it. Nowadays, cooks get a bit skeptical because some clients have found it easier to claim to be allergic to something they don't like, than trying to negotiate substitutions. Restaurants have no option but to take allergy claims very seriously.

Either way, the woman had every right to return the pizza. I quickly prepared another one, instead of picking the artichokes out. If she was indeed allergic, I could be putting her life in danger by not following that procedure. A person with an extreme allergy to gluten told me she could have a dangerous reaction if a cook didn't wash his hands between handling regular bread and her gluten-free one.

I quickly followed the old rule that when the cook screws up, it only takes two minutes to fix. When it's the server's mistake, "Oh my, I don't know; I'm super busy here!" She returned the pizza again, claiming there were still artichokes in it. There weren't. I suspect she confused some of the oyster mushrooms for artichokes. The manager wisely apologized for all inconveniences, putting it all to rest. It's always wise to avoid an argument, so apologize and let it go.

So what was the deal? Did she want a free meal (which she got)? Was she allergic or just averse to artichokes? Her complaint was genuine, at least on the first time around. She and her party left with smiley faces, and it all had a happy ending.

A few weeks later, the manager got a call from another woman, who had been there on a Saturday night with a party of eight. They had a big check with appetizers and entrées, left satisfied, and tipped very well, according to the server. Hours later, they returned for desserts and a few more drinks. The following Tuesday, this lady called the restaurant to say that the meal was horrible. She spoke to one of the managers and, apparently, she used the expression "dog shit" to describe the food. The restaurant is very successful, and the chef had never received a complaint of that sort before. Normally, the chef would make a courtesy return call, but he was turned off by the "dog shit" portion of the reported call. "I just can't start any constructive conversation on those terms," he said.

So, what could have possibly motivated such an outraged call, three days after the meal? We'll never know. Nothing was mentioned to the server or manager on that Saturday night during the usual inquiries of "Is everything alright here?" Maybe she did hate the food and was uncomfortable mentioning it in front of the group. Maybe she had a rough Monday and needed to vent some steam. Maybe she thought it was too expensive and wanted a free meal, to average it down. Who knows?

I believe clients have every right to complain, especially if the food is not what the menu led them to believe or if it doesn't taste good. The menu, in fact, acts like a contract between the restaurant and the client, and the chef should invest good care into writing that document. There is also an implicit agreement that the food will arrive within a reasonable time frame and at the right temperature. Cold soups should be noted on the menu as such to avoid misunderstandings. Restaurants that don't precook the rice for risotto should advise that the luxury of eating this freshly cooked dish will require a wait of thirty minutes.

Common sense and reason should guide your complaints. Were you misled, or did you make a poor choice, overlooking the fact that you don't like sun-dried tomatoes? Was it reasonable to expect that a $5.99 appetizer would be enough food to replace an entrée? Did you order your salad without dressing and now realize that all those leaves are dry like a stack of hay?

Well-managed restaurants should take a reasonable complaint as a good source of feedback on their recipes or the performance of the employees. It is much better to have a client who provides such feedback than one who simply never returns, like me. If it were my restaurant, I would encourage you to give us your feedback. It is frustrating to hang in the kitchen and not know whether people did or did not enjoy what you prepared. You can look at metrics, such as returning clients or increase and decrease in reservations, but direct comments from the clients are much more objective. If the server, manager, or chef is overly defensive or unwilling to receive constructive criticism, too bad for them; they are missing a good opportunity.

What you shouldn't do, as a client, is to call the food "dog shit." This is not a good conversation starter and will not trigger a productive dialogue. You also should not try to engage in a free-food spree. You may be a socialist, who views businesses as a labor-exploiting entity, but you are overlooking the fact that twenty people depend on that entity for their livelihoods, and few restaurants make as much as eight percent profit. Often the owner makes less money than some of the employees. Many dollars and hours were invested in ordering from purveyors, receiving, storing, preparing, and serving your food. It's not free.

# Mother's Day

Anthony Bourdain, among others, has already addressed this, so I'll be brief: Friday and Saturday aren't the best days of the week to eat out. Which days are better? In *No Reservations*, he discusses the schedules of chefs and cooks. The best ones have Sunday and Monday off, so you will find them refreshed on Tuesday. He mentions fresh fish deliveries as one of the factors that could drive your dining decisions, but that will vary based on your location in the country. As a vegetarian, I haven't as much concern about produce aging for a couple of days in the fridge. If too many tomatoes are ripening or too many portobellos were grilled the night before and nobody came because the clients were scared by flash floods, you may find these items in specials the next day, but this is not necessarily a bad thing for you. Specials can truly be an extraordinary treat.

Friday and Saturday are the busiest days for the operation, and it's tough on the kitchen. Most cooks like to be busy. There's a thrill on running four pans at the same time, but it may get to a point when it's ridiculous. When there are three people running the kitchen and we get twenty-five tickets to work on at the same time, we just can't dedicate the appropriate amount of attention to every plate we need to push out. We can't taste the seasoning of every dish, and well, sometimes we may forget one ingredient or another. It's just human. If I would usually take four minutes to prepare a dish and now have to prepare eight in the same time frame, only so much perfection can happen simultaneously. Some of us may even waste some precious time in the kitchen cursing at the stupidity of the manager who allowed a ten-top and a fifteen-top to be booked to arrive at the same time.

Mother's Day and Valentine's Day are two nightmares. No cook I know enjoys working on those days. The workload is ridiculous, way above the capacity of the kitchen. Even if you increase the staff, you still only have eight burners and a two-by-two grill to work with. Lots of things were pre-plated the previous night, waiting in the walk-in to be dressed or (sorry) reheated in the microwave. The menu was reduced to a manageable selection of dishes, chosen for practicality.

The smartest thing you can possibly do is celebrate with your loved ones a week sooner or a few days later. It will be a much better experience: better parking, less waiting, more privacy, and possibly better food. You can probably pay your mom a visit on the second Sunday in May, and think of other things to do with your sweetheart on the actual Valentine's Day evening.

If you must go out on Valentine's Day, you are almost better off going to a chain restaurant. Their food is pre-portioned and frozen anyway, so there's not much room to mess up.

# EPILOGUE

## The Sun Also Rises

In ancient times when I still had a landline phone, I called my phone company asking that the service be transferred to the new location I was moving to. Lisa eagerly handled my call:

—Absolutely, sir. I'll be happy to help you with your request; just a moment please. *If such thing is possible, I believe I could hear her smile.* Since you will be moving to a new area, although it's just a few miles away, we are required to assign you a new number; are you ready to write it down, sir? The number is 215-739-86xx.

—Thank you, but... there is not a single digit repeated in the number. I'll never be able to memorize it.

—Oh, I see, just a moment... How about 215-xx4-2255; no, wait, 215-x33-4411, or I think you will like this one: 215-xx7-7777?

—Lisa, are you new to the phone company?

—Yes, this is my third day! —She sounded genuinely excited.

—Thank you so much, Lisa; I will take the last number you gave me.

Quoting Hemingway quoting Ecclesiastes, "*One* generation passes away, and *another* generation comes... The sun also rises, and the sun goes down, and hastens to *its* place where *it* arose... and *there is* no new *thing* under the sun."

First of all, a curious fact about the Bible: ever since a friend raised the issue to me, I've been intrigued by the random words highlighted in the Bible in *italic*. Sometimes they are innocent words such as *let*, *but*, and *again*, and in other instances they are more profound, such as *power* and *kingdom*. It truly seemed like bad editing by a careless publisher, but I found the explanation that those were words added by the King James's translators to clarify the meaning and give flow to the text. You may find it interesting to know that the Bible once was even harder to understand and didn't flow very well.

The book of Ecclesiastes, which contemplates the meaning of life, is quite beautiful, and can be interpreted on many levels, giving depth to the title of Hemingway's book, in contrast to its characters, who lived rather superficial and frivolous lives. You may be a cynic who chooses to interpret that passage as to signify that no matter what you may think is important in this world, nothing really changes in the long run. Jake and Brett certainly seemed to live like nothing mattered. Or you may conclude that we are so insignificant to the dimensions of the universe that we can't possibly cause an impact. Maybe you take the Buddhist approach that this is a fleeting world and everything is but a cycle.

I prefer the interpretation that there's a refreshed sun coming up on the horizon every new dawn, and maybe it will be a brighter day, that maybe it is our wisdom, that will make the difference. Maybe Lisa, at the phone company, is symbolic of a new momentum in customer service, the dawning of the age when all of those who are assigned to serve the client will, unequivocally, think of my satisfaction first and everything else—including internal processes, rules, and short-term profits—second.

It's not up to anybody but you to make my experience more pleasant and my life a little easier.

Ecclesiastes also says that "… the quiet words of the wise are more to be heeded than the shouts of a ruler of fools." May we all be quietly wise, and that our wisdom overpowers the fools who can't understand the importance of good customer care.